Drinking To Your Health

Drinking

To Your

Health

John A. Ewing, M.D.

 Reston Publishing Co., Inc.
A Prentice-Hall Company
Reston, Virginia

Library of Congress Cataloging in Publication Data

Ewing, John A
  Drinking to your health.

  Bibliography: p.
  Includes index.
  1. Alcoholism.   I. Title.
RC565.E89   613.8'1   81-912
ISBN 0-8359-1474-7   AACR2
ISBN 0-8359-1473-9 (pbk.)

.

© 1981 by Reston Publishing Company, Inc.
A Prentice-Hall Company
Reston, Virginia 22090

10   9   8   7   6   5   4   3   2   1

Printed in the United States of America

A toast to Thalassa

CONTENTS

**Section II   WHAT SPECIAL PEOPLE WANT
                 TO KNOW**

PREFACE

Alcoholic beverages have been around for thousands of years. They have become so much a part of our lives that the term "drinking" has come to mean "drinking alcoholic beverages." Unfortunately, most people who choose to drink alcoholic beverages do so without a proper understanding of the benefits and hazards involved. Everyone deserves to have the facts as they are known to us at present. You need to know so that you can make an informed decision regarding your drinking. In this book I will share with you what I have learned in 30 years of working in the field.

The first section of the book consists of a series of chapters containing information that should be known to everyone, whether they drink or not, but particularly to those who have already chosen to use alcoholic beverages. The second section consists of special chapters for special groups, such as women and minorities. A third section focuses on special topics such as hangovers, sex, and Alcoholics Anonymous. This is a straightforward, no-nonsense book for the average individual who wants to know all that is necessary without detailed documentation or scientific references. However, I have contributed many articles to the scientific literature and have recently coedited and authored a substantial portion of a scholarly book called *Drinking*. Therefore, the fourth section of this book provides information about scholarly and other sources for anyone who wishes to delve more deeply into any specific issues, and it also includes samples of questionnaires. Finally, some pages are provided on which you can keep a drinking diary, should reading this book lead to a decision to monitor your drinking for a while.

Alcohol is man's first and favorite drug. But it is also a food and a poison. The first three chapters of Section I focus on these three aspects of alcohol.

ACKNOWLEDGMENTS

I am grateful to patients, medical students, psychiatry residents, physicians, and colleagues for helping me to organize my knowledge about drinking. I cannot name them all here, but my clinical and research colleagues are co-authors with me of various scientific publications.

Kenneth C. Mills, Ph.D., Assistant Director of the Center for Alcohol Studies, was helpful in providing me with ideas for inclusion.

Elaine Woody, Administrative Secretary of our Center, organized the huge task of getting a typescript prepared; she was assisted by Elva DeBoy, JoAnne Busch, and Lee Ann Owens.

Myra "Sparky" Carpenter, our librarian, and Marjorie

Myers, our Social Research Associate, read all sections with critical eyes and provided editorial suggestions. Mrs. Myers also prepared the index.

Finally, I am grateful to the purchaser of this book, who should know that profits from its sale will help to finance much-needed research studies of alcohol and drinking.

John A. Ewing, M.D.

Drinking
To Your
Health

WHAT
EVERYONE
WANTS
TO KNOW

chapter one

Alcohol

as a

Food

Alcohol is produced when sugars are fermented or broken down by microorganisms such as yeast. Alcohol is found widely in nature, although not in the concentration that can be produced by the chemist. The clear, colorless liquid that the chemist calls *ethyl alcohol* or *ethanol* is basically the same substance that we drink. Undoubtedly, man first discovered alcoholic beverages by accident, possibly by drinking some fruit juice that had been left standing until fermentation had occurred. It is known that the ancient Persians and Egyptians deliberately encouraged fermentation to produce alcoholic beverages. In addition to fruit juices, grains, honey, tubers, and even cactus juice can be fermented to produce alcoholic beverages.

The fermentation process that was used from prehistoric times until the Middle Ages produced wines that contained no more than about 14 percent alcohol because the yeasts are unable to survive in stronger solutions of alcohol. Most beers—produced by fermenting malted grains—have an alcohol content of between 3 and 5 percent. The final alcohol content of a wine depends on the amount of sugar present in the grapes, but it is usually between 10 and 14 percent.

The process of distillation was invented in the Middle Ages. It separates the alcohol and water and enables much stronger alcoholic beverages to be produced. Fortified wines such as sherry, port, and muscatel have distilled alcohol added to them and generally have an alcohol content of about 20 percent. Spirits, such as whiskeys, rum, gin, vodka, and brandy, are produced by distillation of a weak brew or mash, and have an alcohol content of 40 to 50 percent.

Our ancestors devised a means of testing spirits for alcohol content that enabled them to detect any watering down of whiskey. Apart from the alcohol, the other major liquid present in whiskey is, of course, water. It was found that gun powder dampened with a strong whiskey would burn, whereas it would not burn if it were dampened with a weaker whiskey. The term *proof*, then, was applied to a spirit strength that just permitted gun powder to burn. Other spirits were labeled as *over proof* or *under proof*. As used in the United States today, the proof number is precisely twice the percentage of alcohol content. Thus, 86 proof whiskey contains 43 percent alcohol.

Although today's chemists can make alcohol in the laboratory, the alcoholic beverages that we drink are always produced by natural fermentation, with or without distillation. Since foods of various kinds are always involved in the production of alcoholic beverages, it should not surprise us to learn that alcohol is a foodstuff. It supplies energy to the body and can increase fat stores when taken to excess.

"I know that beer can cause a beer belly but you can't get fat drinking vodka," said an intelligent college-educated woman in my presence recently. How wrong she is! A jigger of vodka or any other spirit will supply almost 150 calories, and if it is mixed with sweeteners, it can provide even more. Table 1–1 lists the caloric content of various alcoholic beverages.

If we are trying to lose weight and are watching our overall caloric intake we must allow for the calories in any alcoholic beverages we drink. It is true that some chronic alcoholics who drink a great deal do not seem to gain as much weight as we would expect. However, there are other complex factors at work in such people, including overall poor nutrition and malabsorption of food. Possibly the liver treats the excess alcohol in a special way to produce more heat and less storable energy in alcoholics.

Some national drinking patterns involve using alcohol as a foodstuff while other foods are being taken. The traditional Italian pattern, for example, is one of drinking wine with meals. This is a relatively healthy practice because the absorption of the alcohol is slowed down by the presence of the food solids. If a person wants to feel the effect of an alcoholic drink or two, however, he or she will usually drink it without food because that way it is more rapidly absorbed into the bloodstream and carried to the brain, where the effects are perceived. (See Chapter two, "Alcohol as a Drug.")

Finally, a few words on the use of alcohol in cooking. Alcohol rapidly evaporates when heated, and when wines are

Table 1-1 Approximate Caloric Value for Alcohol in Beverages*

Beverage	Amount	Calories (Kcal)
Beer (4 percent)	12 oz. can	94
Extra strong beer (10 percent)	12 oz. can	235
12 percent table wine	4 oz. glass	94
20 percent fortified wine, such as sherry	2 oz. glass	80
86 proof whiskey	1½ oz. jigger	126
100 proof rum, vodka, etc. or other spirits	1½ oz. jigger	147

*Beer contains carbohydrates which supply about twenty additional calories. Sweet wines supply additional calories because of the sugar content.

used in gourmet kitchens, much of it is driven off by the cooking process. Sometimes a strong spirit will be poured onto food and then ignited, with most of the alcohol being used to supply the flames. In both such instances the flavor will remain, but only small amounts of alcohol may remain in the food when it is eaten.

chapter two

Alcohol

as a

Drug

One dictionary definition of a drug is, "A chemical substance given with the intention of preventing or curing disease or otherwise enhancing the physical or mental welfare of men or animals." Another is, "A habit-forming medicinal substance; a narcotic."

Narcotics are substances that produce a state of sleep or drowsiness, and although alcohol can do this, we do not usually classify it along with narcotics such as opium or heroin. However, as you will see, individuals can become very dependent on alcohol, both psychologically and physically.

Undoubtedly, alcohol is man's oldest drug, and clearly it is his favorite one. Why it is so universally popular (almost 75 percent of all Americans drink alcoholic beverages at least sometimes) is something we will examine in this book. There are social, psychological, and physical reasons for its popularity.

Drugs that affect the psychological state of individuals act upon the central nervous system. The nervous system includes the five senses and is responsible for the perception of all that is going on in and around the individual. Additionally, the nervous system is responsible for actions taken by the individual, for thinking processes, and for a large number of automatic control mechanisms involving the body as a whole.

Alcoholic beverages are often called "stimulants" by lay people, whereas medical professionals usually define them as depressants. If you listen to the noise level at a cocktail party after most people have had one or two drinks, you may find it difficult to believe, as these people talk more and more animatedly and loudly, that they are actually being depressed. They certainly appear to be stimulated! The medical explanation usually offered is that alcohol has removed some of the inhibiting or controlling forces within the central nervous system, thereby releasing more animated and less socially controlled behavior. However, many animals also show stimulation when first given a dose of alcohol, and I believe it is more accurate to say that alcohol has an initial stimulating effect that is followed at higher doses by a depressing effect.

Basically, the reason that people drink is for effects that they perceive as pleasant and beneficial. The word *euphoria* is frequently used to describe a feeling or state of well-being, and drugs that produce this effect can be called *euphoriants*. It seems probable that alcohol's euphoriant effect is due to the fact that it selectively affects various parts of the nervous system rather than hitting them all at once. The first effects of alcohol appear to be upon the parts of the brain that are involved in social awareness, self criticism, and worrying about the future. Thus, it is not surprising that when a person takes a drink or two after a hard day's work he or she will report a feeling of relaxation and a general lightening of concerns. It is only if the drinking goes on that other parts of the nervous system will be affected. For example, an individual might begin to feel tingling of the lips or a numb feeling on the face, which could then be followed by some difficulty in focusing the eyes or in carrying out intricate movements with the fingers, slight slurring of speech, or impaired ability to maintain balance. All of these symptoms, developing progressively and often associated with increasing loss of control of overall behavior, are due to increasing degrees of the effect of alcohol upon the brain. At about this stage, some individuals begin to feel sleepy and will go to bed instead of continuing to drink. Generally speaking, I believe that these are the fortunate ones, because they stop drinking. If they manage to sleep all night and don't feel too bad the next morning, they may have escaped relatively unscathed from the drinking that they did.

More unfortunate, I believe, are those who seem to become more and more excited, talkative, and determined to go on drinking. Such individuals tend to drink more than is good for them at such times and are likely to be involved in some of the complications of drinking that will be discussed later, such as accidents and violence.

Many people set out to have a few drinks (and by a few I mean two or three), which they know, from experience, will contribute to a sense of relaxation, good fellowship, and good feelings. They are in a far different position from the individual who, also from experience, is liable to lose control and go on drinking until, after consuming as much as a pint or more of liquor, he or she may fall into a drunken stupor. Both of these types are seeking euphoria, but only the first type manages to attain it for any length of time. The second type tends to have a bad drinking experience. The only way we can explain the fact that they go back and repeat this again and again is to understand that alcohol impairs the capacity to remember events clearly.

The term *dysphoria* is generally used to mean the opposite of euphoria, namely, a state of discomfort or agitation. Some individuals respond to even small amounts of alcoholic beverages with dysphoria, and this appears to be a physical effect. Orientals generally seem to be sensitive in this way. About 75 percent of all the Orientals who have been studied in scientific experiments demonstrated a greater or lesser degree of dysphoric response to alcohol. Some of my studies have led us to conclude that this is due to the accumulation of a toxic by-product of the breakdown of alcohol known as *acetaldehyde*. Just why Orientals do not get rid of this substance fast enough to prevent it from causing discomfort is not yet clear. It is interesting, however, that the rates for alcoholism are lower in Oriental countries than elsewhere. It would appear that at least some Orientals are less at risk to drink too much because drinking produces discomfort.

Some individuals who are not of Oriental extraction also have a particular sensitivity to alcohol and find that one reaction or another leaves them feeling unable to drink very much or perhaps not at all. Such individuals, if they maintain this sensitivity, would appear to be relatively protected from drinking too much and thus from the risk of alcoholism and the various other complications of excessive drinking.

It has been recognized for a long time that Jews have relatively low rates of alcoholism and problems with alcohol. This has generally been attributed to the fact that they learn to drink wine in religious ceremonies at an early age. However, some of my studies have begun to suggest the possibility of a physical factor as well. Sometimes I give alcohol not by mouth, but directly into the bloodstream. It is only in Oriental subjects and in Jews that I have then seen physical complaints referable to the digestive system even though the alcohol is not being taken in through that system. The studies suggest that possibly such people have a sensitivity to alcohol in part of the brain.

In summary, people drink because they are trying to reach a state of euphoria. Sometimes, unfortunately, they go beyond this stage and become involved with alcohol as a poison.

chapter three

Alcohol

as a

Poison

All living things are made up of one or more cells. It takes billions of cells with many specialized functions to make a human body. All cells that have been studied have been shown to be affected by alcohol, and, in sufficient quantities, alcohol can bring the life of a cell to an end.

Just how alcohol affects the complex workings of cells is still under investigation. Each cell is an immensely complicated chemical factory, producing substances that enable it to perform its function (such as sending messages, in the case of a nerve cell, or changing shape, in the case of a muscle cell).

When we use alcohol as a drug we do so for the immediate effect, and the body system that is concerned with the here and now is the nervous system. Thus, we perceive the drug effects of alcohol through our senses. However, we should understand that all cells of the body are affected by alcohol. For example, even though we are not aware of it, the cells of the body that are involved in making the white and red blood cells are affected by a dose of alcohol. Similarly, the cells involved in healing a skin wound will be hindered in their repair job if alcohol is present in sufficient amount to impair their activity.

All alcohol that is swallowed and absorbed through the wall of the intestine is carried first to the liver, so this organ is exposed to the alcohol in its highest concentration. Not only that, but the liver is then called upon to perform the major work of breaking up the alcohol. Liver diseases of varying degrees are thus commonly associated with heavy alcohol consumption. Even just one weekend of heavy binge drinking can lead to changes in the liver that represent damage. However, the liver has enormous powers of recovery, and a single episode of excessive drinking will not necessarily produce permanent damage. Repeated episodes may lead to accumulated damage. The worst effect of alcohol poisoning on the liver is the disease known as *cirrhosis*, in which parts of the liver are dead or dying and are replaced with scar tissue. Since the liver is an organ that is essential for life processes, alcoholic cirrhosis is a major cause of death.

When the cells of the liver are being damaged by alcohol or other poisons or diseases, certain chemicals escape from these cells into the bloodstream and can be detected at levels that are greater than normal. Thus, doctors have the capacity to perform "liver function tests." Unfortunately, at the present state of our knowledge, we can only detect liver damage after it has become fairly pronounced. Even so, if a doctor reports that the liver functions are impaired, these may return to normal due to regeneration and recovery on the part of the liver if the individual stops drinking.

Another body organ that is quite frequently damaged by heavy alcohol use is the pancreas. Alcohol appears to be directly toxic to the pancreas, and acute attacks are associated with much pain and a substantial death rate.

The stomach, too, is liable to be irritated by alcohol (particularly alcohol in concentrated form), and the lining becomes red and irritable. This may be associated with heartburn, retching, vomiting, and sometimes bleeding.

Muscle cells are also likely to be damaged by heavy alcohol use and this may make itself known by aching, tenderness, and muscular weakness.

The heart is the most important muscle of the body, and it, too, can be damaged by heavy drinking (alcoholic cardiomyopathy). Some physicians believe that unexplained heart failure in young and middle-aged adults is most frequently related to chronic overuse of alcohol. In addition, investigations suggest that mild abnormalities in heart function may occur more commonly in the drinking population than in the nondrinking population.

As indicated in the last chapter, the nervous system is especially susceptible to alcohol, and the function of memory storage is one that may be particularly impaired. Things that occurred during intoxication may not be remembered at all or may be remembered only vaguely. The condition known as the *alcoholic blackout* refers to an episode in which the individual may appear to be acting fairly normally (although obviously intoxicated) but has no memory of it afterwards. I had a patient who awoke in a motel 200 miles from his home and had to go out looking for his automobile before he realized that he had driven from home and checked into the motel by himself. Yet, the last memory he had was of pouring himself a drink in his house. Of course, as I explained in the last chapter, having only vague memories of drinking experiences is a gross disadvantage to an individual because he may therefore believe that he has enjoyable drinking experiences, whereas, in fact, they are periods of relative discomfort and even misery. Indeed, there have been clinical investigations carried out in hospital laboratories showing that alcoholics have far less pleasant experiences when they get drunk then those that they predict. Moreover, later on, after being sobered up, they tend to remember the drinking episode as a much more pleasant one than they reported while it was going on!

These memory distortions may permit the individual to go back to alcohol again and again, seeking the euphoria that is so transient for him.

Other effects in the brain include the fact that the tissues therein appear to adapt to the presence of alcohol quite rapidly, as if to maintain their important life-maintaining functions in spite of the alcohol. This is somewhat like having to rev up the engine of an automobile because the brakes are grabbing. When the alcohol is removed, it is like taking the brakes off, and there is a state of overactivity. To a mild degree, this is what an individual experiences in the form of jitters and "nervousness" on the morning after a night of heavy drinking. To a more extreme degree, this is also the alcohol withdrawal syndrome that is seen when heavy drinkers stop, after days or even weeks of drinking, and it may go on to the condition known as *delirium tremens*. A person suffering from delirium tremens may first have seizures of an epileptic type that are followed by a great deal of shakiness, hallucinations, and frightened feelings. Indeed, in such states individuals have been known to jump out of windows to get away from imaginary fierce animals or persecuting people. Sometimes people die from complications of delirium tremens; the condition is certainly a medical emergency that requires special measures to be taken.

Some long-term brain effects of heavy alcohol use are, unfortunately, relatively permanent. Some of these involve damage to the nerves involved in moving the eyes, difficulties in walking, and a state of mental confusion. This more permanent brain damage seems to be the result of vitamin deficiency, specifically thiamine, one of the B vitamin group. Indeed, it has been suggested that putting thiamine in alcoholic beverages could prevent this type of illness. Unfortunately, all of the other complications, including liver, muscle, pancreatic, and gastric disease would not be prevented by taking vitamins of any kind because they are primarily diseases caused by alcohol poisoning. Also, alcohol may interfere with the proper absorption and utilization of vitamins.

One question that people frequently ask is, "Does even the moderate use of alcohol lead to the killing of brain cells?" The brain is an enormously complex organ that carries out innumerable functions and has lots of built-in "fail-safe" mechanisms. I have just pointed out that some vitamins are essential to brain function and to the structure of nerves themselves. However, does a nightly cocktail or two mean that you are killing off several, or hundreds, or thousands or even millions of brain cells? Many years ago a researcher from South Carolina demonstrated that even moderate drinking could affect the way in which blood cells travel through the microscopic blood vessels of the eye. From this finding he leapt to the conclusion that similar changes in the blood vessels of the brain would lead to an inadequate supply of oxygen and therefore to death of brain cells. This conclusion was widely publicized, including a report in *Readers' Digest*, and it is, as far as I know, the basis for continued concern with this question. The fact is that we have no proof that moderate drinking kills brain cells.

After the brain is fully developed we probably enter into a continuing state of loss of brain cells throughout the rest of our lives. Some of this loss may be due to problems with oxygen supply or various nutrients, and some of it may be due to the relatively minor damage that can occur when physical blows are sustained. I can recall one medical man claiming, although without research proof, that we probably kill off some brain cells every time the head goes through some violent motion, such as when we sneeze. However, nature has provided remarkably efficient packaging for the brain, which floats inside a sort of plastic bag containing fluid, and there are fluid reservoirs inside the brain itself. Thus, I doubt that sneezing can do significant harm.

Not to be forgotten is the process of aging. As we grow older, the reserves within the body gradually become depleted, and it seems likely that aging itself leads to a certain amount of loss of brain cells, with or without alcohol being a factor.

In the case of the chronic alcoholic, there is little doubt that brain damage occurs. Studies that involve putting air into the fluid chambers of the brain and then taking X-rays have shown beyond question that some chronic alcoholics have a loss of brain tissue. This has also been confirmed in more recent studies using the sophisticated and expensive computerized technique known as CAT-SCAN. However, even though it has demonstrated evidence of shrinkage of the brain in chronic alcoholics, the CAT-SCAN technique has also shown some recovery of the shrinkage when drinking stopped.

Chronic alcoholics are generally exposed to injuries beyond those caused by the toxic effects of alcohol. They fall downstairs, bang their heads on various objects that get in the way, and sometimes get involved in fights that may involve blows to the head. The phenomenon of the aging "punch-drunk" fighter who has had a long history of head injuries is fairly well recognized and can develop in the total absence of alcohol use. Thus, as of today, we would have to say that heavy alcohol use may indeed lead to loss of brain tissue and thus loss of mental capacities. However, how much of this is the direct toxic effect of alcohol and how much is contributed by physical injury remains questionable.

No one has demonstrated with scientific certainty that a drink or two before dinner or a few beers in an evening will lead to increased loss of brain cells over and above the loss that is inevitable as we grow older.

chapter four

How

the Body

Handles

a Drink

Let's suppose that you have prepared yourself a mixed drink, or opened a can of beer or a bottle of wine. As you sip your drink, the first thing you do is taste it.

To a considerable degree a taste for alcoholic beverages is something that people learn. Of course, there are certain ways of preparing alcoholic beverages to make them attractive in taste. Very often this involves the addition of various sweetening and flavoring materials. The man who claims that he just loves the taste of bourbon or beer very probably did not like his first taste of the beverage but has learned to associate the taste with the pleasant feelings that he gets from the alcohol. There does, indeed, seem to be a correlation between increasing numbers of women drinking and the availability of the so-called "light" whiskeys and the drinks that "leave you breathless." We also have to wonder if the increased drinking occurring among youth today is associated with the introduction of drinks made to look and taste like milk shakes?

Plain alcohol diluted with water is perceived as slightly sweet, when in the dilutions found in beers and table wines. In other words, many people can detect alcohol at a 4 or 5 percent concentration in water as a sweet flavoring. When the percentage gets up to about 20 to 25 percent, a significant number of people begin to detect a slight burning sensation. Some people reject a mixture with 50 percent alcohol as too burning to put in the mouth, but in taste-testing experiments we have found that others do not complain at all about percentages far, far higher than that.

Of course, there are specific flavors, either added to alcoholic beverages (as in the cocktail) or introduced as part of the natural manufacturing process, that tend to cover the taste of the alcohol itself. The malt and hop flavor of beer is an example: the bitterness covers over the sweet sensation of alcohol. Wines can contain virtually no sugar (dry) or a great deal (sweet). Dozens to hundreds of other chemicals in trace amounts are present in wines and whiskeys, giving rise to the typical flavors of these various beverages. Chemists are studying the complex makeup of wines in order to try to understand why some are more appealing than others.

If the drink that you are holding in your mouth contains enough alcohol for you to perceive it as burning (virtually everyone perceives some burning at about 25 percent), then this will obscure detection of the sweet taste and undoubtedly causes some irritation of the taste buds and other cells lining the mouth and tongue. Remember that distilled spirits contain 40 percent or more of alcohol. If these are drunk straight or without very much dilution, they too, will be perceived as burning. Such a burning sensation must be presumed to represent a cry of pain or discomfort on the part of the cells being touched. An accumulation of injuries of this nature over a lifetime may explain the association between heavy drinking and cancerous processes in the mouth and upper digestive system. However, there are other factors at work, including the tendency for heavy drinkers also to be heavy smokers and the probability that heavy drinkers and smokers in states of intoxication will be more likely to cough and splutter and get a certain amount of alcohol going "down the wrong way."

In general, it would seem to be good common sense to dilute your drinks so as not to produce any unusual degree of burning sensation in the mouth or in the tube leading to the stomach when you swallow.

Finally, while on the subject of taste and flavor, let me point out that within the mouth itself we basically have the capacity to taste only things that are salt, sweet, sour, or bitter. The subtleties of flavor and aroma are detected in the nose. When this delicate instrument is knocked out of commission (such as by a heavy cold) you may not be able to tell the difference between one alcoholic beverage and another.

Now, let's follow the drink down after you swallow it. It is passed on into the stomach and will remain there for a shorter or greater length of time, depending upon various factors. If it is a fizzy-type drink it will pass out of the stomach faster. If the stomach is empty when you swallow that drink, there will be less delay in passing it on to the intestine.

Relatively minor amounts of absorption of alcohol occur in the mouth, the esophagus, and the stomach. The stomach is primarily an organ for digesting food by chemically and mechanically breaking down foodstuffs so that they can be absorbed into the body and used for energy production, growth, and repair. Alcohol does not need to be broken down by digestion because it is already in an absorbable form. Thus, if the stomach is empty the alcohol will be fairly quickly passed along into the small intestine, where the process of absorption takes place. However, if the stomach is already busily occupied with digesting foods when the alcohol arrives, the alcohol will have to take its turn in leaving the stomach. This explains the familiar fact that alcohol on an empty stomach is more rapidly intoxicating than alcohol accompanied or preceded by food.

The intestines are organs that promote absorption of nutrients from the foodstuffs that we swallow. Digestion occurs in the stomach (the saliva in the mouth begins the process) and it continues in a variety of complex ways after foods have been passed from the stomach into the intestines. In the case of alcohol, the molecules of alcohol can pass directly through the lining of the intestine into the blood. A special system (the portal system) is involved in the pickup of nutrients from the intestines since the blood carrying them goes directly to the liver. The liver is the main chemical processing plant of the entire body. The liver controls metabolism, breaks down certain foods, builds up others, and puts others into a storageable form. The liver purifies the blood of many poisonous substances that it may pick up from the intestines. When an individual suffers from liver failure, this simply means that the capacity of the liver to remove poisons from the bloodstream has been overwhelmed, and the person dies from the accumulation of such poisons.

The liver contains a specific substance for dealing with alcohol. The technical name is *liver alcohol dehydrogenase* (LADH); similar substances are found in plants as well as in all other animals. You might wonder why the liver should contain a substance to deal with alcohol, considering that man has only been drinking alcohol for a few thousand years and most animals never drink alcohol. Well, the fact is that even the total abstainer has a certain amount of alcohol in his body. Some of the digestive and metabolic processes can produce alcohol within the body. It has been claimed that within the human being's intestines there is produced daily an average amount of alcohol equivalent to that contained in one quart of beer. Why, then, do people not feel intoxicated? Apparently, whatever alcohol may be made in the intestines trickles to the liver in such small amounts that the liver appears to be able to remove it completely on its first passage through that organ. On the other hand, when we swallow a drink and it is absorbed in the intestines, more alcohol reaches the liver than can be removed on the first pass through. Thus, alcohol gets into the general blood circulation throughout the body and has its primary effect upon the brain.

Recently there has been some publicity in the popular press connected with a man who claims that he suffered from attacks of drunkenness although he never drank alcohol. He claims that American physicians failed to help him and that finally he was diagnosed by someone who knew of the Japanese condition called *mei tei sho*. The name *mei tei sho* means literally "drunken disease" and, according to the believers in this, it represents the fermentation by yeasts within the intestine of carbohydrates that have been eaten. Thus, the man in question claims to have become drunk after eating potatoes or spaghetti. In checking with Japanese physicians about this, I learned that such a condition is reported upon in Japanese medical schools as being theoretically possible, but I have been unable to learn of any studies of a scientific nature that have demonstrated its actual existence. Fermentation of carbohydrates to alcohol takes several days, and if it were going on in the intestine in large amounts it would also cause the production of large amounts of carbon dioxide, and I suspect the individual would suffer more from gas pains and diarrhea than from intoxication! However, I remain sufficiently interested, although skeptical, about such a condition that I would like to see a scientific study of someone who claims to suffer from it. Such an individual would be admitted to a clinical research unit where careful precautions would be taken to make certain that he or she was not doing any surreptitious drinking of alcohol. Then, following blood sampling to show the absence of alcohol in the blood and in the breath, the individual would be given the kind of meal that he or she claims causes intoxication. Thereafter, a series of blood and breath samples would be collected to see if, indeed, any alcohol was being produced and was getting past the watchdog of the body, the liver. Since, to my knowledge, no such study has yet been done I must conclude that *mei tei sho* is an interesting theoretical possibility, but not a reality.

Now, let us return to the alcoholic drink that you have swallowed, that has passed through the stomach, been absorbed in the intestine, and has passed through the liver because the amount was more than the organ could cope with. This alcohol is now in the general blood circulation, and as it goes throughout all parts of the body, its primary effect in terms of what you can detect is in the brain. However, as explained in Chapter 3, it is having effects everywhere. Alcohol, once in the body, is constantly being diluted because it is being mixed with the water within the body, which represents about two-thirds of your entire body weight. (About one-third of your body weight consists of fats and solids.)

Suppose we have a wooden barrel that weighs 50 pounds and contains 100 pounds of water. Then, suppose we pour into that water a known amount of whiskey with a known percentage of alcohol content. We stir the whiskey well into the water so that the dilution is equal throughout the solution; we then have a specific alcohol concentration. This, in effect, is what happens in the case of the human body. The alcohol that gets past the liver is mixed with the water throughout the body, and a certain blood alcohol concentration is reached. This can be expressed as a percentage. For example, if we poured three ounces (two drinks) of 86 proof liquor into the barrel containing 100 pounds of water and then measured the concentration, it would be somewhere between 0.05 and 0.06 percent.

In the case of the human body, however, we are not dealing with a static situation but with a constantly changing one. Even though the alcohol has bypassed the liver and has reached the general circulation, the liver is still working as a chemical factory, burning up alcohol all the time. This burning up process, or metabolism, goes on at approximately the same rate in various individuals. Thus, the alcohol in the entire body is reduced by about 0.015 to 0.018 percent in every hour that passes. Another way of putting it is that, on average, the blood level drops 0.01 percent in every 40 minutes. The livers of some individuals are so used to coping with alcohol that they have increased their capacity to remove this poisonous substance, but such an increase is relatively minor, certainly representing no more than a doubling of the rate of removal. The individual who claims that he has a "hollow leg" has perhaps enhanced his liver rate of removal but also has developed some tolerance within the brain and probably has also learned to pour the drinks down into a stomach that is full of food so as to reduce the rate of absorption into the bloodstream.

Table 4-1 shows approximate blood alcohol percentages

Table 4-1 Approximate Blood Alcohol Percentage

(Illegal to drive if above .10%, shaded area)
Number of drinks (each 1½ oz. 86 proof liquor or 3 oz. sherry or 12 oz. beer)

Body Weight in Pounds	1	2	3	4	5	6	7	8	9
100	.04	.09	.13	.16	.22	.26	.30	.35	.39
120	.04	.07	.11	.14	.18	.22	.25	.29	.33
140	.03	.06	.09	.12	.16	.19	.22	.25	.28
160	.03	.05	.08	.11	.14	.16	.19	.22	.25
180	.02	.05	.07	.10	.12	.14	.17	.20	.22
200	.02	.04	.06	.09	.11	.13	.15	.17	.19

Subtract .01 for each 40 minutes of drinking.
Example 1: 160 lb. man has 6 drinks in 2 hours (120 minutes) = .16 minus .03 = .13%
Example 2: 120 lb. woman has 3 beers in 1 hour and 20 minutes = .11 minus .02 = .09%

Supplied By:

The Center for Alcohol Studies
University of North Carolina
Chapel Hill, North Carolina
27514

related to body weight, the number of drinks consumed within one hour, and the length of time of drinking.

So far, I have talked as if only the liver is involved in the removal of alcohol, and to a considerable extent this is true. However, a certain amount of alcohol does escape from the body through the breath, the skin, and the kidneys. There may also be various tissues in other parts of the body that can break down alcohol, but it appears that the liver does 95 percent of the work.

There are significant differences between men and women when it comes to total body fat content. Compared with men, women have more fat under the skin, which is why women tend to be soft and rounded. On a percentage basis women contain more fat than men. This means, of course, that on a percentage basis women contain less water than men. If a woman and a man of identical weight drink alcoholic beverages of identical amount, these will be diluted, in the case of the woman, with less total water. Thus, she will reach a higher blood alcohol level, and therefore a higher level of intoxication, than the man. This is an important fact that should be recognized by all who are concerned with drinking. It is not reasonable to expect a woman to drink "drink for drink" with a man, since her body is different.

The blood alcohol level that is reached by any individual at any time depends primarily on the size of the drink that they are drinking. Secondly, of course, it depends on the concentration of the drink, since it is possible to buy 80 proof liquors (40 percent), or even 150 proof liquors (75 percent). Thirdly, it depends on the size of the drinker. The larger a person is the more total body fluid he contains, and the more diluted the alcohol will become in his body. Then there is the question of carbonation, since fizzy drinks are absorbed faster and pass through the stomach faster. Food in the stomach holds alcohol in the stomach and delays absorption in the intestine. Finally, there is the question of time; since the liver works at a remarkably constant speed, the number of hours of drinking must be considered. All these factors must be considered in calculating blood alcohol levels. The table of approximate blood alcohol percentage is relatively accurate, however, and can be used as a guideline to indicate what will happen to you when you drink. Drinking coffee or exercising will keep a person awake, but will not affect blood alcohol levels or sober him up.

Before leaving this complex subject let me make a few comments about breath testing. A variety of studies have shown that there is a fairly consistent relationship between the levels of alcohol found in the breath and that in the bloodstream. The official conclusion is that breath levels represent twenty-one hundredths of the levels found in the blood. Thus, when a person is asked to blow into a breath testing machine, that instrument is detecting the amount of alcohol in the breath and then the reading is translated into the amount in the blood. In most of the United States the level above which it is illegal to drive a motor vehicle is 0.1 percent. A look at Table 4-1 shows that this is fairly generous, since, for example, a man weighing 180 pounds could have four drinks within one hour in order to reach that level. Some countries have lower levels. In Canada the legal limit at the present time is 0.08 percent, and in some Scandinavian countries it is as low as 0.05 percent. Remember that your body (mainly your liver) can remove alcohol at the rate of approximately 0.015 percent per hour. Thus, if you weigh 160 pounds and drink four drinks in one hour, you could still be just below the legal limit at the end of one hour because of the fact that your liver factory has gone on working.

The reader who has been exposed to medical or laboratory training may be more familiar with the "milligrams percent" method of reporting blood alcohol levels. The following table is provided to show the equivalents:

0.01%	=	10 mg %	=	10 mg per dl (100 ml)
0.05%	=	50 mg %	=	50 mg per dl
0.10%	=	100 mg %	=	100 mg per dl
0.25%	=	250 mg %	=	250 mg per dl

chapter five

Availability and Cost Factors That Influence Drinking

Perhaps you are lucky enough never to have had to worry about the bill when you have been drinking in a bar or ordering bottles in a store. However, there are many studies indicating that cost is a factor that influences how much some people drink and therefore affects overall consumption levels. Nature provides alcohol and man merely harnesses the useful services of the yeasts, then bottles and markets the final product. The actual production costs of alcohol are relatively low. However, governments have always been prone to tax anything that is regarded as a luxury and particularly anything that at least some people treat as a necessity. Federal, state, and sometimes local taxes are imposed on alcoholic beverages and represent a significant contribution to government income. Needless to say, governments are frequently tempted to increase the tax, but then the danger of diminishing returns has to be considered. In the case of alcoholic beverages in particular, there is the possibility that bootleggers and moonshiners might find it more and more attractive to provide illicit sources of what people want to drink. In certain parts of the United States moonshining has been common, particularly in the Appalachian region, but even there the activities of these lawbreakers seem to be diminishing. The fact is that, compared to the overall cost of living, it is becoming relatively less expensive to drink. Although there have been minor increases in the prices of alcoholic beverages during the recent inflationary surges, these are proportionately small compared with the price of other essentials such as a loaf of bread, a pound of tomatoes, or an automobile.

Studies have shown that when there is a sudden increase in the price of alcoholic beverages there may often be a sudden decrease in alcohol consumption and related problems. For example, on the Island of Trinidad, Professor Michael Beaubrun has shown that dramatic drops in automobile accidents exactly coincided with significant increases in the price of rum. However, as the cost of living continues to rise and the relative price of the rum diminishes, one quickly sees a return to the previous levels of rum consumption and highway accidents.

Some studies have shown that the consistent rise in consumption as the relative price of alcoholic beverages goes down is followed some years later by a rise in the rates of liver cirrhosis. This is not surprising, since, as explained in the last chapter, alcohol is a major cause of cirrhosis.

State taxation practices vary a great deal, so that in some states it is quite expensive to drink beer, while in others beer may be cheap relative to the price of wines and spirits. A more realistic approach that should be encouraged would be to tax all beverages at relatively the same amount, proportionate to their alcohol content. The reason poor, down-and-out alcoholics are often referred to as "winos" is simply because such people generally take their alcohol in the form of cheap fortified wines. Such beverages are relatively less taxed than beers and spirits, and therefore the drinker gets more drunk for each dollar he spends.

Nearly every time that I have been quoted in newspapers or interviewed on television or radio about alcohol drinking and alcoholism, I have received letters from well-meaning citizens who insist that, "If you didn't sell alcohol to people they wouldn't drink it and there would be no alcoholism." Unfortunately, this conclusion is too simplistic and quite at odds with the experience in this country during the "noble experiment" of Prohibition. Although at that time it became illegal to sell alcoholic beverages, and thus to drink them, it quickly became clear that this was not a majority wish of the people. Indeed, finding ways of getting around the law contributed to the development of organized crime, much of which is still with us today.

Nevertheless, there is some role for government control with regard to such things as availability and cost. For example, it seems reasonable to control the number of outlets available. Likewise, governments can probably encourage less damaging drinking practices by promoting the sale of alcoholic beverages where food is consumed. Having specific ages under which it is illegal to purchase, and therefore to consume, alcoholic beverages is also probably wise and will be discussed in later chapters. Generally speaking, the role of the government can be most useful if it is aimed at promoting "healthier drinking practices." This is not to say that there is any such thing as clearly identifiable "healthy drinking." This entire book is aimed at providing the reader with an overview of drinking in all its aspects with a major emphasis on identifying the less healthy aspects of drinking so that you can make informed decisions about drinking. An unhealthy drinking pattern is one that promotes drinking for the sake of drinking, since it is likely to promote more drunkenness and heavy drinking. Thus, making alcoholic beverages available with food, at sports events and as part of family activities may well be "less unhealthy" even though it is not necessarily "healthy."

chapter six

Social Factors

That Influence

Drinking

We live in a drinking society, indeed in one that I have sometimes called the "I-need-a-drink society." Drinking is all around us, even if we never go into places where drinks are served. It is virtually impossible to open a magazine without seeing advertising for alcoholic beverages. Even though spirits are not advertised on radio and television, many television shows portray drinking and thus communicate something to the viewer about it. A recent study of soap operas revealed that pouring, mixing, and drinking drinks is a common way of filling these afternoon dramas.

In general, advertising tries to convey messages to make the viewer want to try the product. In the case of alcoholic beverage advertising, one hears from the promoters that all they want to do is change one's choice of brand. Understandably, the promoter of Brand A would be happy to see those who drink Brand B give that up and turn to Brand A. However, I am unaware of any scientific studies that have proved that this is all such advertising accomplishes. It may be, for example, that it persuades some people to drink Brand A whiskey instead of Brand C soft drink.

Those who prepare advertising are very skilled at conveying particular messages. Thus, the average viewer of most liquor advertising gets the message that it is smart, cultured, and attractive to use certain alcoholic beverages. Some advertising says rather bluntly that the use of alcohol can contribute to sexual conquests, just as Ogden Nash said many years ago:

> Candy
> Is dandy;
> But likker
> Is quicker.*

The old adage "Birds of a feather flock together" is very applicable when it comes to drinking. Heavy drinkers tend to associate with heavy drinkers and light drinkers often have other light drinkers for friends. To a considerable extent, behavior is molded by one's peers and the way that they behave. Physicians who are trying to determine how much a patient drinks will often get a more honest answer if they ask the patient about how much he thinks his friends drink.

A number of ingenious ways have been devised to measure alcohol consumption. In most countries the government has records of the alcoholic beverages produced, and it is possible to calculate how much on average is consumed by each individual or by each person of drinking age. Such reports, of course, do not take into account any illegal production that might go on. However, illegal production and consumption are virtually nonexistent in many countries. France has had

---

*From *Verses From 1929 On* by Ogden Nash. Copyright 1930 by Ogden Nash. First appeared in *The New Yorker.* By permission of Little, Brown and Company.

the highest per capita consumption rate for quite some time, but this has actually dropped slightly since World War II. Even so, France was still the leader until very recently when it was overtaken by Portugal. In the case of some other countries, even some geographically close to France, there have been dramatic increases in alcohol consumption since World War II. For example, in the Netherlands consumption has doubled; but it still has quite some way to go before catching up with France. Reasons for such trends are difficult to identify and are the cause of much speculation.

When dealing with individuals, or groups of individuals, researchers rely upon a variety of methods. Sometimes researchers will watch drinkers in bars and try to record how much they are drinking over what period of time. But obviously only very limited samples can be made of this nature, and the results are not applicable to other drinkers in other situations. A common technique is to ask people about their drinking habits in terms of whether or not they have drunk any alcoholic beverages in the last week, or the last month, or the last year. A variety of special procedures such as the "quantity frequency index" is involved, and while we know that not all responses will be accurate, these techniques do permit a certain amount of comparison between one part of the country and another, or between particular groups.

There is a general tendency for people to drink more in cities than in rural areas, and for drinking to be associated more with higher social class, more education, being male, and so on. By defining drinkers as people who drink alcoholic beverages at least once in a year, it has been shown that almost 75 percent of adult Americans can be so classified at the present.

Anyone who wants to learn more about social factors and ways of measuring drinking in various social groups should turn to the specialized literature listed in Section Four of this book. Meanwhile, don't forget that even though there are differences in drinking practices in different parts of the nation, and in different social groups, the problem of alcoholism knows no boundaries. It spares no social class, no work category, and no type of individual. Alcoholism occurs among housewives, blue collar workers, physicians, airline pilots, priests, and nuns. The only people who do not suffer directly from alcoholism are those who are total abstainers. This is not to say that I advocate total abstention; there are social and personal reasons to identify some beneficial aspects of drinking. However, anyone who drinks is at risk for developing problems from their drinking and this may go on to alcoholism as we shall see.

chapter seven

Psychological

Factors

That Influence

Drinking

The psychological makeup or "personality" of any individual represents the final outcome of a variety of factors. Some of these are the inborn genetic potentials inherited from previous generations that determine such things as intelligence, level of energy, and vulnerability to special problems such as mild attacks of feeling "down in the dumps," severe depression, schizophrenia, or other mental illnesses. Also, contributing to our psychological makeup in a major way are the environmental influences of parents, other children in the family, teachers, neighbors and similar significant persons.

Overall personality varies greatly from individual to individual: some people are confident and self-assured while others greatly lack this asset; some people are constantly bothered by fears and anxieties while others have no such concerns. The interesting thing about alcohol is that, within limits, it seems to be able to wipe away many of the concerns and anxieties of bothered people. To call alcohol a psychological panacea is no exaggeration. Many scientific studies have demonstrated how alcohol can resolve doubts, anxieties, and conflicts that exist within individuals.

For example, a man may have some concern about himself as a man. This may not take the form of conscious concern about his masculinity, but may be present as vague doubts or may only be expressed when the defenses are down, as in dreams during sleep. The interesting thing is that alcohol seems to provide a temporary sense of self-confidence. I do not necessarily mean that under conditions of intoxication a man will more actively pursue a sexual conquest with a woman. He may do so, but it is equally possible that he will not bother to seek a conquest because the alcohol provides by itself enough reassurance to the individual about his sexual identity and capacity.

If we accept the fact that the "typical male attitude" is one of aggression and competitiveness, then we see that alcohol drinking, particularly in amounts above the level of light drinking (more than two or three drinks) spurs loud, competitive, aggressive, and sometimes even violent behavior.

What about the woman who has doubts about her sexuality? Here again, there are studies indicating that alcohol can provide relief. Under states of intoxication, women experience more fantasies of being womanly. It has been shown that women alcoholics have more probability of a history of experiences that could provide them with doubts about their femininity.

Alcohol can give individuals other effects that will be perceived as benefits. For example, the individual who feels tense or nervous and who loses this feeling with alcohol is liable to keep drinking in the future when faced with tension provoking situations.

Other studies have shown that people in a state of frustrated aggression are likely to drink more, apparently because they are "uptight" about someone else and unable to deal with these feelings directly. For example, a man may have been bawled out by his boss in an unjustified way. Perhaps he cannot deal with the boss directly without risking losing his job. Thus, he is "burned-up" and tense and fuming inside. At such a time he is more likely to drink more if, when he turns to alcohol, the alcohol contributes a sense of relief; and drinking becomes something he does again and again, anytime he is filled with feelings he has been unable to express.

There is even some evidence that alcohol can, for a while at least, serve to overcome feelings of psychic depression. Here I am talking about the individual who feels sad either because of some experienced loss or, in the absence of some external precipitant, because of a built in tendency to feel despondent from time to time. Alcohol is not a strong antidepressant drug such as physicians can prescribe today for depressed people. However, it is not a prescription drug and I often see patients who have been "treating" themselves with alcohol for depressive diseases. Getting them off the alcohol and on to better medications is the obvious way to go.

One's individual response to alcohol is important in all these considerations. Some people tend to have a euphoric response to alcohol whereas others tend to respond with dysphoria or "the blahs." Just how alcohol affects the brain and nervous system as a whole is still under active investigation. What we can say today is that it selectively affects sections of the brain and seems to do so by inserting itself into membranes, thus affecting the passage of chemical messengers from one area to another. There are also other mechanisms involved, such as the hormones or chemical messengers, which pass from one part of the body to another through the bloodstream. It is possible that the recently discovered endorphins are also involved in the mechanism of alcohol euphoria. The endorphins are important because they are substances made within the brain that appear to have vital functions in terms of mood and pain perception. The discovery of endorphins was spurred by the mystery of why areas of the brain (known as receptor sites) could be occupied by molecules of a plant substance (such as opium, morphine, and heroin) that only get into the human body under artificial conditions. The possibility that the body made its own morphine-like substances led to the successful search for the endorphins. Thus, the word *endorphins* refers to morphine-like substances made within the body. Some recent animal findings indicate the possibility that endorphins do participate in alcohol responses. But some human studies that I have recently undertaken have failed to confirm this.

In the year 1970, two different groups of research workers published papers indicating that substances very much like opium and morphine might be elaborated within the body during states of alcohol intoxication. It was initially shown that these substances could be made in the test tube when certain brain chemicals were mixed with acetaldehyde, the first breakdown product produced by the burning of alcohol within the body. Other studies have now confirmed that these chemicals, known as TIQs (tetrahydroisoquinolines), can be found within the living body under special circumstances.

Quite recently, my colleague, Dr. Robert Myers, has taken incredibly small amounts of these TIQs and injected them into specific portions of the brain of laboratory rats. Rats so treated have shown a remarkable change in their willingness to drink alcohol when it is provided as an alternative to water in the rats' cages. Indeed, some animals so treated with the TIQs have begun to drink alcoholic beverages with about the same intensity as the human alcoholic. Much work remains to be done in this area, but already we are faced with the question: Is it possible that TIQs accumulate in the brain of the chronic alcoholic, making him crave more alcohol? This does seem to be a significant possibility, and, if it can be proved, would lead to the next question: Can we find antidotes that remove this craving in the experimental rat and can similar antidotes be given to alcoholic people?

As you can see, although this chapter started out discussing psychological factors, that is, the feelings that people have about themselves, I have ended by talking of the interplay between psychological factors (such as behavior toward alcohol) and chemical factors, some of which might be inborn. The truth is that we cannot separate human behavior from human chemistry any more than we can separate the brain and the body.

chapter eight

Inborn Factors

That Influence

Drinking

Benjamin Rush, one of the signers of the Declaration of Independence, also known as the father of American psychiatry, knew that alcoholism ran in families. Indeed, this tendency has been noted again and again by medical men over the centuries. Needless to say, some people have viewed this as due to "the bad seed" whereas others have seen this as the result of children following the bad example of their parents. The argument of whether it is a question of "nature" or "nurture" has been going on for a long time and only recently has the evidence come out strongly in favor of nature.

The term *nature* refers to the inborn or constitutional components of an individual, as opposed to *nurture*, which refers to the environmental influences on an individual.

Just a few years ago the general feeling seemed to be that nurture was the more important factor when it came to alcoholism. After all, proponents argued, an alcoholic father or mother sets a very bad example, and it is an example that the children are likely to follow when they grow up.

Arguments favoring a constitutional component come from studies of twins, half-siblings, and adoptees. There are two kinds of twins, identical and nonidentical. Identical twins are of the same sex and possess identical genes, meaning the blueprints whereby their bodies were formed. Thus, in addition to looking identical they share common blood types and body chemistry. We know from studies of development that identical twins come from the same single fertilized egg and thus are also known as *uniovular* twins. Nonidentical twins, on the other hand, are the result of two separately fertilized eggs and therefore may be of different sex and are usually relatively different in appearance. Interest in a variety of diseases has led to studies of twins because a disease that carries a major genetic or inborn component is more likely to appear with the same frequency in identical twins than in nonidentical twins. This, indeed, has been demonstrated to be so in the case of alcoholism. If one of a pair of identical twins is an alcoholic, the probability of the other one also being an alcoholic is over 50 percent. In nonidentical twins, the probability of both having the same illness is significantly lower.

Half-siblings is a term used to describe half brothers or sisters who have either a father or mother in common. Studies of half-siblings have shown that a child of an alcoholic parent is more likely to become alcoholic than a child raised in a household with an alcoholic step-parent.

What these studies demonstrate, in effect, is that biological inheritance is more crucial than parental influences within the household.

The most convincing findings of all come from studies of children who were adopted in Denmark. These were initiated by Dr. Donald Goodwin and colleagues and probably could not have been accomplished in many other countries where adoption records are kept very confidential. The people studied were males under the age of 30 who had been adopted within the first six weeks of life. By checking back into records they identified a group of 55 who had had an alcoholic parent (nearly always the father) and these were compared with 78 adopted children for whom no alcoholism was known in the biological parents. Goodwin and his colleagues, in fact, set out to disprove once and for all that there could be an inborn tendency towards alcoholism. A psychiatrist interviewed all of these young adult adoptees without knowing which ones came from alcoholic families and which ones did not. Likewise, the people being interviewed did not know anything about the parents who had put them up for adoption. Their own histories in terms of drinking and problems with alcohol were carefully researched, including not only upon what they reported, but also hospital and legal records.

The findings of this study proved to be both surprising and convincing. In the case of these Danish males, there was clear-cut evidence of significantly more problems with alcohol and treatment for alcoholism in those whose biological parents had suffered from the disease.

Clear-cut evidence of a similar biological factor in females has not yet been produced. However, there are at least four additional studies that have now been published, all of which support the findings of Goodwin and his group. Thus, we can say that there is a strong case, based upon these adoption and other studies, for there being an inherited component in at least some instances of alcoholism.

Before going further, we must consider the possibility, indeed the probability, that there is more than one type of alcoholism. As an analogy, let me point out that there are many types of various diseases. We could take diabetes as an example. One form of diabetes comes on early in life and may be due to some viral or other infection that knocks out the insulin-producing cells of the pancreas. Other types come on later in life. Some are severe and difficult to control, requiring daily injections of insulin, whereas others simply require a modified diet. One type of diabetes develops as a result of obesity.

In a similar way, I believe that we will eventually have to understand alcoholism as comprising a variety of conditions.

Some people become careless drinkers just as others are careless eaters. One objective of this book is to help the careless drinker to establish more control. It is also my hope to help the alcoholic who cannot establish control to recognize this fact and to choose to make some informed and intelligent decisions about what to do.

While it may be that there are several types of alcoholism, for the moment let me suggest that we simply consider two that we will call "primary" and "secondary." The concept that there are some "primary alcoholics" who have some kind of biological predisposition to have trouble with alcohol has been around for quite some time. Those who do not fit the primary category would be thought of as "secondary alcoholics," who have started to use alcohol injudiciously and to excess because of the relief that it gives them for their depression or anxiety or other psychological problems. It is even possible to conceive that secondary alcoholism could develop in an individual who obtained relief from a physical symptom, such as pain, from drinking.

A psychologist working in a hospital in New Jersey, Dr. Ralph Tarter, decided to divide a population of alcoholics going through his treatment program into primary and secondary categories. Primary alcoholics were those for whom there was no known precipitating cause for their excessive drinking plus at least six of the following eight characteristics: (1) increased tolerance for alcohol; (2) experience of withdrawal symptoms when alcohol use is stopped; (3) euphoria after first drinking experience; (4) euphoria with first drink following a period of abstinence; (5) no history of social drinking; (6) abnormal drinking before the age of 40; (7) problems with alcohol before the age of 40; and (8) loss of control. Those patients who did not meet the criteria to be classified as primary alcoholics were simply considered to be suffering from secondary alcoholism.

When Tarter and his colleagues looked back into the childhood history of these patients, they found twelve items that significantly differentiated the primary alcoholics from the secondary alcoholics as well as from psychiatric patients and healthy people. Childhood characteristics that were associated significantly with the later development of primary alcoholism were daydreaming, feeling left out, being impulsive, working below ability, being easily frustrated, having trouble sitting still, being unwilling to accept correction from authority figures, having poor handwriting and a short attention span, problems with fidgeting, not completing projects undertaken, and being generally regarded as "overactive."

The interesting thing here is that a very similar list of childhood characteristics was developed from studying the school records of the Danish alcoholic men that I have described above.

Overactivity in childhood has become recognized as a specific condition sometimes also called the *hyperkinesia syndrome*. It may be that such children are delayed in the maturation of their nervous system, and of course various theories have been put forward, including that they are suffering from food allergies or are sensitive to trace amounts of preservatives in food. Investigations of the condition are continuing but we already know that such children have problems with short attention span, and are distractable, restless, and generally more irritable than their classmates. A variety of other studies that looked back upon childhood characteristics of alcoholics have reached very similar conclusions. This raises the possibility that there may be certain biological factors that make such people more likely to turn to alcohol for some sense of relief. It might be, for example, that such individuals, compared with others, have a heightened sense of tension and general discomfort about themselves that may be relieved significantly by swallowing alcohol.

Some researchers, such as my colleague, Dr. Tom Gualtieri, are already asking the question, "Are alcoholic patients hyperactive children grown up?" Sophisticated brain wave testing and other procedures are called for to answer this question, and, most importantly, it will be necessary to study specifically those who appear to be "primary alcoholics," rather than to look at alcoholics as if they were all the same.

A great deal of research remains to be done before these issues can be clarified, but already we have enough information for specific individuals to make important personal decisions.

For example, if you have a family history of alcoholism, and if, as a child, you fit the description of the hyperactive child, then you can reasonably reach the conclusion that you are probably likely to have trouble with alcohol should you use it. Any such individual who has not yet started to drink alcohol should think twice before starting. If you meet these criteria and already drink, then you are certainly someone who should do very careful evaluation and monitoring of your drinking, such as is described later in this book. If you have an inborn tendency to have trouble with alcohol, you may feel that nature has dealt you a dirty trick, but in fact you are much less at a disadvantage than someone who has inherited diabetes, for example. Such an individual has problems in coping with sugars and yet cannot totally avoid sugars in the diet. The person who has trouble in coping with alcohol *can* totally avoid alcohol in his or her diet. If you feel that life without alcohol is not worthwhile, then you need to spend some time with people who have devoted themselves to the program of Alcoholics Anonymous. Here you will find those who have proved to themselves that life without alcohol can be highly rewarding and even better for them than when they were drinking.

Being forewarned of the possibility of alcoholism is relatively simple when there is a marked family history of alcoholism in one or more preceding generations. However, a necessary condition is the actual consumption of alcoholic beverages. It is possible, therefore, that you may have inherited a significant potential for alcoholism and yet have no family history. For example, perhaps your father had a predisposition to become alcoholic, but, because of social, religious, or cultural values, chose never to do any drinking.

There is another pattern that I have seen in several families, namely that alcoholism appears to jump generations. One Swedish study showed that even the grandsons of alcoholic men had a significantly greater probability of developing alcoholism themselves when compared with the general population. The pattern that I have seen involves an alcoholic grandparent whose children do not themselves drink. This may be because they were disturbed by their father's drinking and decided not to drink themselves. In each instance, there has been a typical "conspiracy of silence" when it comes to telling the grandchildren about the life and death of the grandfather. His alcoholism is not mentioned, and the children start drinking themselves without any awareness of the possibility that they have an inborn predisposition to have trouble with alcohol. I hope that, having read this book, parents who find themselves in this same situation will feel less stigmatized by the fact that there is a family history of alcoholism and will feel free to tell Mary or Johnny about their grandfather who could not handle alcohol.

Before leaving the subject of the inborn factor, let me point out that we must do further research to identify how this factor has its effect and what is passed from one generation to another. It may be that the inborn factor is not the specific tendency to have trouble with alcohol but whether or not one has a euphoric or dysphoric experience with drinking. Some of our studies have looked at an enzyme found in the blood (DBH) that reflects, to some extent, the activity of the sympathetic nervous system, and we have shown some correlations between this enzyme level and how people respond to alcohol. There must be other factors of an inborn nature remaining to be elucidated. In Chapter 7, I mentioned the work of Dr. Robert Myers with TIQs; the possibility exists that some people get rid of these substances when they are formed, whereas in others they accumulate, producing a craving for alcohol. As we get more and more knowledge and understanding there will be potentially new ways of helping the person who has trouble with alcohol. However, we do not have to wait for these discoveries to evaluate our drinking and to make informed decisions about it.

chapter nine

Some

Advantages of

Drinking

Television personality Ed McMahon was recently quoted as saying, "Drinking is God's reward for hard work." I certainly agree that alcohol is Nature's gift to mankind and a gift that can be used safely by many, but not all, people.

What are some of the personal advantages that drinking can provide? At a purely personal level many people enjoy the sense of relaxation and well-being that one or two drinks can provide. If the drinking is done at an appropriate time and place, for example at the end of the day's work, and if it is done in sensible amounts, it can make a contribution to the quality of life for many people. The phrase "quality of life" should be kept in mind because it refers not only to personal responses but also to interpersonal relationships. If a few drinks make a man feel relaxed but at the same time make him become unpleasant to his wife or children, the quality of life for these people is not being enhanced by alcohol. Later I will discuss some of the warning signs of dangerous drinking, but at the moment let me emphasize that using alcohol to relax and feel more carefree after a heavy day is only appropriate if it is done in a limited degree. The individual who stays drunk all evening is damaging the quality of his life significantly, even if we ignore the potential health hazards. Feeling carefree for an hour or so while relaxing with a drink is quite different from using alcohol to escape from necessary decisions, actions, and things that one *should* be worrying about.

It is appropriate to say that drinking can even contribute to better health. A little judicious drinking, even on a daily basis, may not only make you feel better but may in some way, not yet fully understood, contribute to better health. The question of whether drinking could shorten or lengthen life is one that has interested scientists for a long time. A famous biologist, Raymond Pearl, published a book in 1926 called *Alcohol and Longevity.* His findings have never been disproved. He constructed life tables for various groups of individuals ranging from total abstainers through moderate drinkers to heavy drinkers, classifying people according to both drinking frequency and amount. His study showed that moderate drinkers had a lower mortality rate than abstainers, and, among men, moderate steady drinkers had lower mortality rates than heavy occasional drinkers.

There are other studies that demonstrate similar findings. Insurance companies' studies deal with a self-selected group, namely those who apply for insurance and therefore are not necessarily representative of the entire population. Likewise, companies select those whom they want to insure and thus their findings are not universally applicable. However, insurance records indicate that policy holders about whom there is adverse information concerning their drinking have significantly higher death rates, ranging from two to five times greater than standard groups. The death rate is particularly high in people who do "spree drinking" and are in the younger age groups. These are people who go on binges or benders in which they drink a great deal over a relatively short period of time; such episodes may be interspersed by periods of no drinking. This pattern clearly differs from that of the individual who has a couple of cocktails before dinner.

Studies of patients suffering from alcoholism consistently indicate much higher death rates than in other people. These deaths are not due only to the effect of alcohol upon the body; the leading causes are accidents, poisoning, violence, and suicide. Some studies indicate that the alcoholic is about 30 times more likely to commit suicide than the normal individual. Even among young alcoholics, mortality rates exceed those of the general population. One study of young Navy and Marine Corps alcoholics showed that those who had been treated in hospitals for the disease had a death rate seven times higher than nonalcoholics of comparable age in the same military services. A variety of community studies demonstrate the effect of drinking on mortality. One study in Massachusetts showed higher than normal death rates in both abstainers and "high volume drinkers." A California study showed that heavy drinkers among younger men have a higher than average mortality rate. There was a slight tendency for light drinkers to show the lowest mortality when the figures were adjusted for age. One government report provides similar evidence indicating that, in terms of overall frequency of drinking, the lowest mortality rate in each sex and age group is at an intermediate level of drinking. Under the age of 60, the highest death rates occur at the highest frequency of drinking. Above the age of 60, the highest death rates are among abstainers. In that study, what is called "frequent heavy drinking" is measured by the frequency with which an individual drinks five or more drinks on one occasion. Such relatively heavy drinking is so rare among women over 50 and men over 60 that mortality rates could not be calculated. Among younger subjects, an increased mortality rate does appear to relate to frequent heavy drinking.

Heavy alcohol use is associated with death from "natural causes" as well as violence. The excessive use of alcohol, especially when combined with tobacco, has been implicated in the development of certain cancers of the respiratory tract and upper digestive system. Nonwhite men appear to be especially

susceptible. Then there is the issue of alcohol and the heart. *Alcoholic cardiomyopathy,* discussed in Chapter 3, is clearly due to the heavy or excessive use of alcohol. However, there is evidence that alcohol is *not* a significant risk factor when it comes to heart attacks of the more common type known as *myocardial infarction* or *coronary thrombosis.* Indeed, some studies indicate that moderate alcohol use may actually be associated with a lower risk of such a heart attack. Research carried out in Hawaii and Massachusetts points to the possibility that light drinking, even on a daily basis, is associated with higher levels of what are known as *high density lipoproteins* (HDLs). The HDLs are apparently helpful when it comes to cholesterol, a substance that we cannot avoid because it is present in many dietary substances and is also manufactured by our bodies. Cholesterol is a necessary foodstuff and a substance that the body uses to make many other vital chemicals. However, lining of arteries with cholesterol appears to be a major reason for blocking the blood supply, and if the heart muscle does not get blood, it dies. HDLs appear to assist in moving cholesterol from the lining of blood vessels to the liver, where the cholesterol can be broken down. Much more has to be learned about these important relationships, but for the average light or moderate drinker, the benefits of drinking may tie in with the HDLs. Let me emphasize, though, that there are certain inborn disturbances of fat metabolism that are worsened by alcohol intake. If your physician tells you that you suffer from a condition requiring abstinence from alcohol, the way to insure personal longevity is to take his advice.

Before leaving the discussion of advantages of alcohol, it is necessary to mention that it is an excellent social "lubricant." People who would otherwise be shy and diffident often become more relaxed and secure in social situations involving alcohol. The usual rules of social behavior are relaxed when alcohol is being served; a book called *Drunken Comportment* by Mac-Andrew and Edgerton points out that alcohol is the signal for "time-out behavior." When drinking, people are less inclined to stand on ceremony and are more able to relate freely with each other. On the other hand, continued drinking to the point of too much can lead to excessive loss of control, regrettable statements, and even violent behavior. Anyone who feels that alcohol is "essential" to a social gathering should drop in on an Alcoholics Anonymous meeting. There you will discover that people can be loving and lovable without a drop of anything stronger than coffee.

In Chapter 7 I described how certain inner conflicts such as hidden doubts and/or fears about one's masculinity or femininity could be assisted by alcohol consumption. This, too, is an advantage of drinking but it is also a potential danger. If an individual does a small amount of drinking to feel better about himself or herself for a limited period of time, no particular harm is done. However, if that person uses continued, frequent, and excessive drinking to avoid dealing with these inner issues, then a state of suspended growth or delayed maturation is brought about. Under such circumstances, the advantage of drinking becomes a significant disadvantage.

chapter ten

Some

Disadvantages of

Drinking

The individual who never takes an alcoholic beverage throughout his or her lifetime cannot develop alcoholism. This is true even should there be major constitutional and/or psychosocial predispositions toward developing alcoholism. Looking at the other side of the same coin, we must recognize that he or she who chooses to drink is also accepting risk, however small, of developing alcoholism. Statistically, that risk is always present but may be much greater in some individuals than in others. As an overall figure, I think it is reasonable to say that there is about one chance in twelve that, if you drink alcoholic beverages, it may cause problems either throughout your life or at some point in your life.

The probability of becoming hooked on alcohol is always

there for anyone who uses it, yet, as I have demonstrated, for many people the moderate use of alcohol is such a contribution to the quality of life that they consider the risk worth taking. If you are not yet a drinker, consider whether or not you tend to be moderate in your lifestyle with regard to other things or whether you tend to go overboard. People who have difficulty in controlling their use of other substances (food, candy, coffee, tobacco) are more likely to have trouble controlling their use of alcohol.

Each time we take a drink, the phenomenon of tolerance is put into play. As the alcohol is used up, the brain cells may be in such a state of excitability that they seem to be calling for another dose of alcohol. This, undoubtedly, is a mechanism seen to a major degree in individuals who are daylong daily drinkers. It has been described, for example, in peasants in wine growing countries who receive part of their compensation in the form of generous volumes of wine. An individual may start off with wine before breakfast, in addition to wine with all meals, and perhaps a dose every hour or two. Such a person feels extremely uncomfortable if the supply dries up, and can be expected to undergo a greater or lesser degree of the withdrawal syndrome that was described in Chapter 3. There are significant dangers in remaining in this state of slight intoxication all the time: the major medical concern is the state of the liver. That organ has many other functions to perform in addition to burning up alcohol, and it may be that certain toxic substances will accumulate because the liver is so busy taking care of the alcohol that it cannot attend to the other substances. The likelihood of developing liver disease is significantly increased when the liver is not given a rest from its alcohol-destroying duties.

But, you may ask, what about me? I never take a drink in the morning or indeed all day, but when I leave work I stop off at my favorite bar and have two or three drinks before I go home. Another common pattern is for the individual to go home and have two or three drinks there before dinner. In later chapters we will discuss the question of amount of alcohol being consumed. At the moment, let's look mainly at the issue of habit formation.

Is your habit of having a few drinks at the same time every day, and usually in the same place, so deeply ingrained that you begin to feel positively uncomfortable if it is not gratified on schedule? For example, if you have to work late in the office, does not having your drink on time cause you any discomfort or even a sense of dismay? If you change time zones by flying from east to west, can you delay your predinner drinking until it is dinnertime, or do you find yourself hitting the bottle in midafternoon?

What I am trying to say is that there is nothing particularly bad about habits themselves, provided we have some control over them. It is the habits that control us that are dangerous. One of the disadvantages of drinking is that the habitual drinking may go out of control. Later on, in Chapter 15, when we discuss self-monitoring, I will show you how to evaluate your control of your habit versus your habit's control of you.

The classic pattern of the North American alcoholic (as opposed to the wine-growing peasant who drinks all the time) is one of repeated attempts to get his or her drinking under control. For example, he or she may conclude that whiskey is the problem and may therefore turn to gin, vodka, or beer. Since, as we know, the problem is not the type of drink but the interaction between that individual and the alcohol, such attempts at regaining control are doomed to failure.

Alcoholics are unhappy drinkers. Not only do they frequently have unhappy experiences during their drinking, but they are unhappy, and guilty, about their drinking. Most conscientious and intelligent people (and many alcoholics are typically both) will be self-critical when they find themselves unable to control an important aspect of their lives. For many years they may have been boasting to themselves or others, "I can take it or leave it," until finally they make the decision to leave it (for a while at least), usually because some crisis has arisen. Perhaps a spouse is accusing them of being "an alcoholic," or they were arrested for driving under the influence, or they did something particularly embarrassing during a blackout. The classical pattern is one of success, for the time being at least. As long as our alcoholic has decided to do "no drinking until July 4th," or some other distant goal, he will often be successful. Meanwhile, he feels that he is building up justification for future drinking because friends or family can no longer accuse him of being an alcoholic: he has "proved" that this is not so by going for months without a drink.

In Chapter 35, on questionnaires for detecting drinking problems, you will see that this pattern of "going on the wagon" has repeatedly been identified with drinking problems. Those who are personally involved with an alcoholic should reject bargains involving "going on the wagon to prove I am not an alcoholic." I will have more to say about this in Chapter 24, addressed to friends and family of alcoholics.

I have dwelt at some length on the subject of loss of control because it is so important. What are other disadvantages of drinking? Most important are the evidences of damage to the body. If, at any time, a physician has evidence that drinking is threatening your health in any way or is worsening some disease process that you already have, then, without doubt, you should take this as an indication that your drinking days are over. It is unfortunately true that some physicians try "the scare technique" with alcoholics, promising them dire consequences if they go on drinking. Many of my alcoholic patients have described being exposed to this and then going on to outlive the physician who made the prediction that, "You'll be dead in six months if you go on drinking." I know, and I wish that all physicians knew, that statements of this sort tend to force the alcoholic to drink more than ever. After all, if you respond to anxiety by drinking, what will you do if someone deliberately makes you more anxious? Thus, my advice, given above—to stop drinking if there are good medical reasons—is aimed at the intelligent reader whose physician has found some well-documented justification for giving this advice. If your physician has laboratory evidence for the existence of liver damage, problems of diabetic control, certain types of metabolic diseases, heart, nerve or muscle damage, then discuss things with him or her very seriously. If the physician can present you with convincing evidence, then the next question is whether you should abandon drinking for all time or just for some months. Again, only an intelligent doctor-patient discussion addressed to your specific case can lead to a correct decision.

There are other disadvantages of drinking that may be presented directly to the drinker without the intervention of a physician. A relatively common experience, for heavy drinkers at least, is loss of control over behavior, leading to actions or words that are later greatly regretted. This includes not only driving under the influence of alcohol and violent behavior while intoxicated, but also common accidents—large or small—around the house, inappropriate and embarrassing behavior at parties, violence between spouses, angry outbursts, and so on. If you have lapses of memory such that you cannot believe that you did what people say you did, then you have suffered an alcoholic blackout. This is a sign of drinking too much and is a warning of further alcohol problems to come. If you have experienced an alcoholic blackout and cannot bring your drinking down to a level where you never experience one again, then you should take this fact as evidence of needing help with your drinking problem. See Chapter 26.

There are certain ways in which the body indicates that it is being subjected to abuse of one kind or another: pain and discomfort help the body to protect itself. Thus, if you have a strained muscle or tendon in your leg, you will find yourself limping in such a way as to minimize further damage to these tissues while they heal. The same is true when the body cries out following alcohol abuse. This may be in the form of a hangover (see Chapter 28), or just some slight shakiness on the morning after some heavy drinking (a manifestation of the withdrawal syndrome). In such states, you should recognize that your body is responding to abuse and you should take the message.

One particular form of such a message is recognized by physicians as the "holiday heart syndrome." Following holiday weekends, physicians may see patients whose hearts are beating irregularly (cardiac arrhythmias) due to the toxic effects of high levels of alcohol in the blood.

There is a relatively rare condition that also represents a significant disadvantage of drinking known as "pathological intoxication." It has been well documented in a variety of clinical studies that some individuals pass into a state of loss of self-control at relatively low levels of alcohol consumption. Some such individuals display abnormal electrical brain impulses when low levels of alcohol are present in the bloodstream, while others show no such evidence, at least not any that is measurable with today's techniques. With or without the measurable brain changes, however, such individuals may become grossly violent or act very inappropriately, sometimes with only a vague or absent recollection of what occurred. It seems quite likely that some violence and even murders can occur in states of pathological intoxication. Less dangerous but embarrassing things can also happen. I know an 18-year-old girl who deliberately kicked a police car in such a state. When tested at the police station, her blood alcohol level was well within the legal limit for driving an automobile. Another case involved a young man who propositioned a policeman and got himself arrested.

My advice to anyone who has any hint that they may be reacting in this peculiar manner to alcohol is to avoid drinking altogether. If even one or two drinks may, at least on occasion, lead to this extraordinary loss of personal control, then the time may come when some episode occurs that is more than embarrassing. I have examined one man who killed his wife in what was probably a state of pathological intoxication. The law does not recognize such a condition as justifying illegal behavior. If you have a history of drinking a few drinks and then acting irrationally without control, and perhaps without memory, you are at risk to repeat this in future drinking episodes. Thus, any time you choose to drink you must be perceived as choosing to take the risk of ending up in prison. As I will show you in Chapter 32, it *is* possible to lead a happy and fulfilling life without alcohol, and if you think that you have experienced pathological intoxication my advice to you is quite simple: "Don't drink again."

chapter eleven

Warning

Signs

of Dangerous

Drinking

In previous chapters I have discussed a variety of conditions that will now be listed here as warning signs of dangerous drinking.

The first group of warning signs are those that relate to overall health. Here we must include documented evidence presented by an understanding physician with appropriate laboratory tests for alcohol-related disease or alcohol-worsened disease. Then, there are the warning signs that the drinker's own body presents to the drinker: shakiness, severe hangovers, blackouts, postdrinking palpitations, depressed feelings associated with drinking, anxiety attacks associated with drinking, digestive disturbances, sleep problems, and so on. Another warning is the development of tolerance to alcohol: this means needing to drink perhaps twice as much as you used to in order to achieve the same effect.

Next, there is the question of your personal functioning. Has drinking interfered with your performance of anything in any way? Do you find yourself drinking more than you intended? Performance relates to your entire life activity, but one of the most important activities is your work. Do you think that your work has deteriorated in any way because of drinking? Have friends or family ever raised this possibility? We will come back to this issue in Chapter 35 when we look at ways of identifying personal problems with alcohol.

At an interpersonal level, a significant sign of dangerous drinking is some form of personality change associated with drinking. At the extreme we could be talking about a "Dr. Jekyll and Mr. Hyde" switch. At less extreme levels, however, we may find the husband or wife who becomes foulmouthed while drinking, or who attacks the spouse verbally or physically, perhaps even in the presence of the children. Children are very sensitive to some of the personality deteriorations that alcohol may bring about in some individuals. I have heard the children of alcoholics say things such as, "Mom is no fun to be around when she is drinking," or, "Dad always seems to be mad when he's had some drinks."

Another warning sign that drinking has become obligatory, and thus dangerous, is if it takes precedence over other needed expenditures. Are you buying alcoholic beverages instead of foods because you cannot afford both, for example? The purchase of alcoholic beverages should be regarded as a luxury to be indulged in only after the essentials of housing, clothing, and family well-being are attended to. If these things suffer because of alcoholic purchases, then this is dangerous drinking.

chapter twelve

How Risky

Is Drinking?

Now that we have considered some of the advantages and disadvantages of drinking as well as some of the warning signs of dangerous drinking, we are ready to consider the overall question of risk in relationship to drinking. I have shown that alcohol is three things in one: a food, a drug, and a poison. As a food, alcohol in itself poses no particular risk unless one depends too much upon it as a source of calories. In this case, its incomplete nature as a food becomes a problem because the individual who is drinking but not eating lacks essential nutrients, particularly vitamins. However, it is as a drug and as a poison that the risk issue primarily needs to be examined. Alcohol, the drug, releases types of behavior that normally are kept in check. If a person merely becomes overtalkative or boisterous when drinking, this may not be particularly risky, but if he displays a tendency to show bravado, takes physical risks, or becomes prone to violence, then the drinking is quite risky. Alcohol, the drug, makes people careless. There are particular situations in which one cannot afford to be careless; this especially is true when hazardous machinery is involved. Don't forget, too, that although alcohol is a major factor in highway unsafety (see Chapter 29) and drinking while operating complex machinery is clearly very risky, nevertheless there are undoubtedly many thousands of home accidents that are related to drinking. The person who has been drinking often has a careless attitude and is perhaps impaired in balance and is liable to trip, fall downstairs, fall off a ladder, or otherwise add to the statistics of domestic injuries while intoxicated.

There is one relatively rare, but very sudden and usually fatal, risk, often called the "cafe coronary" that is often associated with drinking. The victim chokes on a piece of food that has been inadequately chewed and that "goes down the wrong way," leading to blockage of the air-passages to the lungs. Such individuals do not die of a coronary, but may give the appearance of having had a sudden heart attack. Unless quickly treated, the victim dies of suffocation. The National Center for Health Statistics records about 3,000 such choking deaths annually. A most effective treatment for this has been developed and utilized on numerous occasions: it is called the *Heimlich Maneuver*. The helper gets behind the choking individual and puts his arms around him, grabbing one hand around his other fist and pushing upward on the diaphragm at a point between the tip of the breast bone and just slightly above the navel. An individual can even perform the procedure upon himself to dislodge the piece of food by blowing it out with the pressure of air in the lungs. As of mid-1979, Dr. Henry Heimlich, who developed the technique in 1974, had received almost 1,200 letters attesting that it was a life-saver.

Still on the subject of risk, we must consider the risks involved in exposing organs such as the liver, heart, and brain to alcohol. There is evidence that continuous low levels of drinking going on over days, weeks, months, and years are associated with more damage to vital organs than is found in nondrinkers. Thus, the peasant in the wine-growing area who is partly paid with large volumes of wine, which he drinks, is found to have a significantly higher level of liver disease. The next question that a drinker may then ask is, can he save up his drinks; for example, instead of having one or two drinks each night, have a blast by drinking one or two quarts of spirits over the weekend. This "spree drinking" (described in Chapter 8), is a dangerous type of drinking that has been proven to be associated with inceased mortality.

The overall conclusion has to be that there is always a certain risk with drinking; indeed, there are few human activities that are totally devoid of any risk. The question becomes one of trying on a personal level to evaluate the risk and to minimize it to whatever you find to be an acceptable level for yourself.

A very recent Swedish study showed that alcohol was the most important single factor associated with death at about the age of 50. An alcohol positive history was present in over half the men who died. There was evidence that these men were heavy drinkers, based both on chemical tests and history. This goes to show that while light drinking may be beneficial, it is easy to overdo alcohol intake and end up with a greater than normal chance of premature death.

chapter thirteen

Examples

of Risky

Drinking

Continuous drinking that goes on all day long and for days on end or even weeks or months is risky, primarily because of the risk to vital organs in the body. Even though you may be able to drink on such a schedule and yet rarely feel or act intoxicated, still your organs are being affected.

Loss of control drinking is also dangerous. Here we are talking about sprees, benders, or binges that may be indulged in either by the careless or ignorant drinker or the alcoholic drinker. People who fall into the first two categories may be able to learn to drink in a more moderate and less risky way. Certainly, becoming careful and monitoring one's drinking is much to be recommended. Likewise, those who are ignorant about the dangers of drinking can become informed by reading a book such as this. For the "primary" or "essential" alcoholic, however, at the moment I have no promises or encouragement to provide in terms of being able to be a controlled and safe drinker. Help for the alcoholic is described in Chapter 23, which discusses how to be a total abstainer.

A variety of experiences that may be associated with drinking represent warning signs that the drinking is risky: these include hangovers, memory blackouts, aggressive behavior (either verbal or physical), and personality changes that are painful to others.

Even the "three martini lunch" that we have heard a lot about in recent years can represent risky drinking, particularly if the martinis are consumed on an empty stomach before the lunch is started. Most normal drinkers find that heavy drinking such as this during lunch leads to a significantly reduced work potential for the rest of the working day. The drinker who can swallow three martinis, then eat lunch and perform as well in the afternoon as he has in the morning is showing some evidence of developing a tolerance for alcohol.

Drinking before physical exercise is probably risky. Studies have shown that various organs are affected by alcohol, particularly the cardiovascular system. The work of the heart is impaired by exercising during intoxication. Thus, if you are going to jog or swim or exercise in any way, it is best to postpone drinking until after the exercise.

I have already mentioned drinking while handling dangerous machinery, including the automobile, but keep in mind that there are other ways of taking risks. For example, in one large British city a third of all pedestrians killed in road accidents had been drinking; many of the males had blood alcohol levels that would have made it illegal to drive a motor vehicle. My colleague, Dr. Page Hudson, who is Chief Medical Examiner for the State of North Carolina, has even more impressive data showing that 63 percent of pedestrians killed had alcohol in their blood, with the levels averaging 0.27 percent. It is equally risky to smoke, particularly in bed, when drinking. Of 100 fire victims, Dr. Hudson found alcohol present in 75 percent, with the average level being 0.26 percent. An individual with such a blood alcohol level is very likely to doze off to sleep, and a cigarette can set the bedclothes to smoldering, leading to death from smoke inhalation.

Of 100 drowning victims, Dr. Hudson found alcohol present in 58 percent with the blood alcohol levels averaging 0.19 percent. Even such an apparently safe activity as swimming may be made significantly more risky by drinking alcohol. It may be that under such circumstances some individuals lose their sense of balance and are unable to swim to the surface once they go under.

Dr. Hudson has even shown that the victims of both knifings and shootings are significantly more likely than not to be intoxicated. On the average, you are more likely to be murdered by a drinking "friend" than by a strange gunman.

One form of extremely risky drinking is when drinking is combined with drugs that have similar (depressant) effects on the brain. This includes certain tranquilizers, sleeping pills, and a variety of other medications, particularly anything that makes one sleepy or less alert. This combination can be a killer, or, if it does not kill, it can leave a person with permanent damage or in a Karen Ann Quinlan type of coma. When you take a medication, read the instructions carefully. If you have any doubts about whether or not it is safe to drink with the medication, ask your doctor or pharmacist. Some medicines interfere with the capacity to recall what has happened. A possible sequence of events is for the individual to take some pills and then some alcohol, and then later in the night, perhaps after some sleep, to wake up and take more pills and possibly more drinks, with virtually no recollection of the earlier dosage. The cumulative effect of all this could be never to wake up again.

A variety of personal problems can also point to risky drinking if they are associated with drinking. If you have sleep problems, depression, anxiety, phobias, social problems, memory problems, nameless fears, or feelings of being persecuted, and you drink, any one or a combination of these *may* be the outcome of your drinking. There is one way to find out, and that is to enter a period of total abstention from alcoholic beverages. An adequate trial would require going for at least two or three months without alcohol. If at the end of that time the symptoms that were previously bothering you have disappeared, you have good evidence to attribute them to the alcohol. (How to go about starting an experimental period of abstinence is discussed in Chapter 15.)

chapter fourteen

How Much

Drinking

Is Totally

Safe?

The key words in the question, "How much drinking is totally safe?" are "totally safe," since, when you examine the question, it becomes apparent that virtually no activity that we undertake is totally safe. Even things that we do not normally view as dangerous cannot be labeled totally safe. For example, we have not yet devised a totally safe flight of stairs, because every now and then someone falls down them. Is there a totally safe rate for driving an automobile? You might be inclined to think that an automobile traveling at 5 miles per hour is totally safe, but vehicles traveling no faster than that have killed people. It is fairly clear, however, that we are willing and able to identify certain speeds as being generally unsafe and thus we set speed limits. In a similar way, it is relatively easier to identify generally unsafe levels of alcohol consumption than to identify generally safe levels. A variety of medical and epidemiological studies have led some experts in the field to identify the daily consumption of 80 grams or more of alcohol as hazardous. However, one recent French study of the development of liver cirrhosis shows an increased risk for this disease at a daily consumption of 60 grams for men and only 20 grams for women. Because nearly all the studies that I refer to are based on the metric system, Table 14-1 shows the approximate number of grams of alcohol in a variety of alcoholic drinks. Keep in mind that this is an approximation and that it assumes that you are drinking measured drinks. For example, a mixed drink of spirits contains one jigger of 1½ ounces. If you are drinking "doubles" you must allow for that.

Now, if we take the 80-gram figure as representing more or less the grey zone between "probably less hazardous" and "probably more hazardous" drinking, there is still the question of individual susceptibility or immunity to the risks of drinking. As of today, we have no means of predicting in advance by any scientific study the capacity of people to exceed 80 grams a day safely. It may well be that there are some individuals for whom a safe level is much less than 80 grams a day (of course in the case of the alcoholic, I have already emphasized that he or she can consume no alcohol safely).

Decisions about drinking have to be made on a personal level similar to the way that, on a national level, decisions are made about driving. Since driving is clearly a hazardous activity, we limit permitted speed, and yet, since it provides a

Table 14-1 Approximate Weight of Alcohol in Various Beverages

12 oz. can of beer	12 grams
16 oz. can of beer	16 grams
2 oz. fortified wine (port, sherry)	9 grams
4 oz. table wine	10–12 grams
1½ oz. 86 proof spirits	15 grams
1½ oz. 100 proof spirits	17 grams

highly desirable mobility, we accept the risk that this relatively generous speed limit permits us to take. Most of us accept the risks of driving because of the benefits therein. Do you find enough benefits in your drinking to accept a certain level of risk? For some individuals there really is no question, since they have religious or moral scruples against drinking and against the use of mood-changing drugs in any form. Others find that alcohol provides more discomfort or dysphoria than "highs" or euphoria and therefore decide that it is simply not worth it. However, for the majority of people, alcohol does seem to provide a significant surcease from the day's tensions, relief from nagging doubts and worries, resolution of inner conflicts, and so on. Now, on an individual level, you have to decide if the benefits for you outweigh the risks.

A friend and colleague, Dr. Ulf Rydberg, of Sweden, once tried to survey the literature on this topic and to come up with a paper defining a safe level of drinking. He, too, noted the 80-gram figure but decided that in order to provide a "safety factor" he had to divide the figure by 10. Thus, he concluded that if a person is to use alcohol on a daily basis and wants to have some kind of guarantee that it is safe, this can probably be accomplished by a daily intake of no more than 8 grams. The flaw in such an approach, however, is that 8 grams of alcohol will do so little for most people as to be equivalent to almost no drinking at all. It would mean opening a can of beer, drinking two-thirds of it and pouring away the last one-third. Yet, as a conscientious physician and alcohol expert, Dr. Rydberg felt that this figure was the only one that he could identify as "safe."

Back in the nineteenth century, a British physician named Anstie also evaluated this question and expressed the belief that a safe level of drinking that would not cause disease was the equivalent of 1.5 ounces (about 35 grams) of alcohol per day. This would be, for example, three ounces of 100-proof whiskey, or half a bottle of wine, or three cans of beer. He emphasized that this should be taken with meals and that the whiskey was to be well diluted, an important point to keep in mind.

Nowhere in this book have I produced evidence to indicate

Table 14-2 Tips for Safe Drinking

- When taking a drink, remember you are taking "a fix" of your favorite drug.
- Determine in advance how much you are going to drink and never exceed that.
- In regard to your drinking, always think of moderation and keeping watch on how much you have had.
- Use a jigger to measure spirits (the heavy-handed host who pours generously for his guests or himself is doing no one a favor).
- Spirits should be diluted with a mix.
- A beer with lunch may be all right, but the two- or three-martini lunch spells danger.
- Avoid the mixes of two different alcoholic beverages such as martinis, Manhattans, etc.
- Sip and savor your drinks—don't gulp them down.
- Eat something when drinking (the one possible exception would be when you are having no more than two small drinks in the twenty to thirty minutes prior to dinner).
- Limit the length of time of your drinking—stop after an hour or two.
- Perceive getting drunk as something to be guilty and worried about.
- Do something else when you are drinking—like having a conversation or reading.
- Regard drinking as something to enhance life, not as a remedy for boredom or "having nothing to do."
- Always have soft drinks and food available for your guests.
- Remember that the host who pushes drinks is a drug pusher.
- Regard a hangover as a definite warning that you were drinking too much the night before. Remember, though, that some people *can* drink too much and never suffer a hangover.
- When you feel "I need a drink," this is the worst time to drink.
- At a party, sip the first drink over thirty minutes and do the same time for the second; stretch the third drink out until you leave; never take a fourth.
- Surprise yourself occasionally by doing something else when you otherwise would have had a drink—take some exercise, or a hot bath, or some fruit juice.
- Never use alcohol in the morning to get you going or to fight a hangover.

that daily drinking in itself is unsafe. What does appear is that continuous drinking all the time is unsafe and heavy sprees (five or more drinks at one time) are unsafe, whereas the levels of "social drinking" indulged in by most individuals are not in themselves dangerous, *provided* the warning signs of risky drinking and the other disadvantages of drinking are not present. Keep in mind that your drinking will be safer if it is accompanied by food and try to keep it as a secondary, although important, aspect of your life if you choose to drink. In other words, the person who lives to drink is giving alcohol too large a position in his life pattern. Safe drinking seems to be drinking that is used to enhance the quality of life for the individual; unsafe drinking is drinking that is the goal in itself.

chapter fifteen

Making an

Informed

Decision About

Drinking

This chapter is the kernel of this entire book. It is preceded by basic information without which you really cannot make an informed decision. You may already be a total abstainer, a moderate drinker, or a heavy drinker: but, unless you have devoted a great deal of time to studying the topic, you probably made your decision on grounds other than factual information.

If you have already decided to remain a total abstainer for all of your life, it still is desirable for you to know the facts and opinions that I am presenting in this book. Perhaps you will be in a position to provide necessary information to drinking friends or acquaintances. Perhaps you are in a job where much of this information is necessary.

If you have already begun to drink, then now is the time

to reappraise your drinking in the light of the preceding chapters. If you have turned to this chapter before reading the rest of the book, by all means finish reading the chapter. But don't then put the book aside; that would be a cop-out. Read the preceding chapters and any of the following ones that apply to you and then tackle the issue of "What will my decision be?"

I have not made this the final chapter because I feel that there are some special issues that need to be addressed by people under special circumstance. Thus, this "kernel" chapter is followed by chapters that provide information about special age groups, special types of drinkers, and special circumstances, such as drinking and sex. These following chapters could be read by you before or after making a decision about your personal drinking. If there is a chapter that specifically applies to someone like yourself (for example if you are a teenager, a woman, or believe you are already suffering from alcoholism), obviously, you should read that section before making your informed decision.

Now, let's look at the background for your informed decision. I have demonstrated that there is basically no such thing as "riskless drinking." Thus, the first question you must ask yourself is, "Do I get enough enjoyment and benefit from drinking to justify subjecting myself to the risk?"

The next question is the issue of amount and type of drinking. You already know about the toxic properties of alcoholic beverages, about how alcohol is diluted in the water of the body, and how the amount of water present correlates with body size, sex, and obesity. You know that relative risks increase as amounts consumed increase, and you have heard about "Anstie's limit" and other ways of judging consumption. If, based on this information, you can clearly identify yourself as a low-level drinker (even though a regular one), you may decide not to change your pattern of consumption in any way. However, you most certainly should monitor it over the years to be careful that you do not creep into bad habits, increasing consumption and perhaps beginning to experience some of the disadvantages of drinking.

If the preceding information makes it clear to you that your drinking is beyond the level that could be called moderation for you, then you are faced with the issue of setting a lower limit for yourself and seeing whether you can maintain that. One way of watching your drinking is by keeping a diary; Appendix A of this book provides such a diary.

If, having read the preceding Chapters, you are still not sure how to classify your drinking, then you should consider monitoring it for some weeks or months by using the diary in Appendix A. Once you have this information accumulated, you will be in a better position to return to this chapter and to decide whether or not you need to do anything about your drinking.

In addition to the issue of amount, there is the question of on what occasions do you choose to drink and what happens. I hope that you already understand that even daily drinking, if moderate and limited in amount, cannot be typified as particularly dangerous in itself. There may even be health benefits. Clearly, for many people there are psychological benefits, which is why they return to drinking again and again. However, remember that continuous daily drinking, meaning drinking over many hours, is risky, just as is binge or heavy episodic drinking.

I have surprised some of my medical student classes by pointing out that I personally drink more than some of my patients who are chronic alcoholics! This is based on annual consumption totals. The point is that such patients spend significant periods of time in jail or in hospitals or rehabilitation centers. Also, many alcoholics are typically binge drinkers who "go on the wagon" for weeks or months at a time. In a year, such a patient may consume only a few gallons of spirits and/ or beer. For comparison, let's take the moderate but daily drinker who has just one 2-ounce cocktail before dinner: this alone adds up to almost six gallons of spirits annually. Let's say that he drinks two cans of beer most nights, and perhaps three on Saturdays and Sundays. Such a drinking pattern could hardly be called immoderate or excessive, assuming that the individual has no health complications. Such a drinker never gets intoxicated to any significant degree. Yet, in addition to the spirit consumption listed above, he is also consuming a hundred gallons of beer annually.

Finally, in looking at your own drinking, consider its effects. Is there any evidence that you are suffering from bad effects? Does your physician give you a clean bill of health, are you free of any psychological symptoms, and are you enjoying life to the hilt? Have there been any drinking episodes associated with behavior that you later regretted or felt guilty about? Has anyone close to you had reason to express concern either about the amount you are drinking or about personality changes associated with drinking? Have you had any legal problems in connection with drinking behavior?

Cutting back

If your self-inventory has led to the decision that you ought to cut back your drinking, this can be done quite safely. For example, a person who has been drinking three or four mixed drinks before dinner and then spending the rest of the evening in a semi-stuporous state, usually with several more drinks, may decide to have only two drinks before dinner and perhaps only one more before bedtime or a couple of beers during the evening. Making a firm resolution to cut back and keeping a record of success and failure is likely to be all that you need to do. If you fail to be able to cut back, then you must face the question of why is this so. Conceivably, there are reasons within yourself and within your environment that make a semi-stuporous state each evening seem attractive. For example, perhaps you are bored, having few hobbies or other interests. Perhaps you are living in an unhappy marriage and are using alcohol as an escape. Perhaps you have sexual hangups and are using alcohol to avoid dealing with these. Perhaps you are filled with frustrated anger and turn to alcohol for relief. If you can identify factors that may be making your drinking go out of control, then the next question is, can you do something about them? If you cannot identify such factors, some time spent with a counselor such as a marriage guidance expert, a psychiatrically trained nurse, a competent clergyman, a psychologist, or a psychiatrist may be well spent.

You will find further suggestions about controlling your drinking in the following chapters, and you will also find in Chapter 34 a list of suggested sources of outside help.

Sometimes a person who is already drinking at an extremely heavy level makes a decision to cut back. This could be an individual who is drinking more than a fifth of gin or whiskey a day. For such a person to stop suddenly can be uncomfortable and even occasionally dangerous because of the possibility of convulsions and delirium tremens. Quite frankly, a person who has reached the level of a pint or more of whiskey daily (or equivalent in other beverages) is drinking dangerously and probably alcoholically. However, such drinking could be the result of long-developed careless and ignorant drinking. If you are an alcoholic who wishes to stop, then see Chapter 23. If, however, you are not ready to identify yourself as alcoholic and want to see if you can drink in a more logical fashion, then remember what I call "the 10 percent rule." This simply states that you can safely drink 10 percent less each day until you reach the level that you want to cut back to. Let's say that you are drinking as much as a quart of spirits daily. Most drinkers could not consume that amount, but some of my alcoholic patients actually have done so over long periods of time. Admission to a hospital for "drying out" is always a possibility (see Chapter 26). However, for the "do it yourself" drinker, taking 10 percent less each day over a period of several days will avoid discomfort and danger from withdrawal. For example, the daily drinker of one quart (32 ounces) needs simply to decide to drink 3 ounces less on the first day of the withdrawal plan. The 29 ounces can be spread over approximately the same length of time as was the quart. The next day, the goal should be 26 ounces. Day three allows 23½ ounces, Day four 21, Day five 19, Day six 17, Day seven 15, Day eight 13½, Day nine 12, and so on. If you can successfully follow this regimen, please note that by Day thirteen you have safely, and relatively comfortably, reached 7 ounces per day, which probably has brought you out of the dangerous drinking zone. Of course, there may be problems with what to do with the time that you are no longer "zonked out," or you may find that not being intoxicated so much leaves you with other problems for which you might need some counseling or other outside help. The greatest danger for someone who has been drinking this amount and who succeeds in reducing it is that he or she will become careless again or begin to provide the various rationalizations that seem to justify "just a little bit more." In that regard, keeping a drinking diary over months or years or even for the rest of your life may be very helpful.

Stopping altogether

If it is your informed decision to stop drinking altogether, either permanently or for a planned time, the 10 percent reduction rule described above can be applied below the moderate level until the daily consumption is zero. If you have tried that and find that you cannot accomplish it or that your drinking creeps back up, then you need some outside help. This could involve asking your physician to prescribe some medication to assist you in dealing with any tension or other emotional state that seems to prevent your stopping altogether. However, you and your physician should know that people who have trouble with controlling their alcohol consumption tend to have trouble with controlling the amount of medication they take, particularly when the medication is one such as the minor tranquilizers that show cross-tolerance with alcohol. I have a psychiatrist friend who is a recovering alcoholic and who became hooked on one of these tranquilizers. "For me," he says, "that tranquilizer was just like powdered alcohol."

If you and your physician will keep this warning in mind, a few days of medication can sometimes be justified. For others, particularly if the drinking has been heavy and prolonged, a visit to a drying out hospital or center can be helpful. Some of these are attached to hospitals or alcoholism centers and provide nursing and medical care. In recent years, "social setting detoxification centers" have been developed, and these provide a great deal of emotional support ("tender loving care") without giving medications, although medical backup or transfer to a medical facility is always possible. It is remarkable how people who were dependent on large volumes of alcohol can stop all at once when they are away from their regular environment and surrounded by supportive caregivers.

Regaining and maintaining control

If you are an alcoholic with a history of alcoholic drinking patterns (particularly if there is a family history of alcoholism and if you were a hyperactive child), it may be completely unrealistic for you to hope to regain control of your drinking. Abstinence may be an easier alternative. Almost certainly you have tried a variety of things such as changing what you drink, going on the wagon, making promises to yourself and others, and so on. To be honest and fair to yourself, it is best for you to turn to Chapter 23.

If the information provided so far leads you to conclude that you have developed careless patterns and that you might yet regain and maintain control, then read on.

Your first decision must be to keep a drinking diary; it will give you a record of change, something concrete to focus your attention on, and, I hope, something to be proud of. It's also useful to do this in conjunction with other people. Maybe you and your spouse would decide to lower your drinking together to a new set level. You do not necessarily have to aim for the same level. For example, if you are a 180 lb. man, you may decide that you will limit yourself to 8 ounces of spirits daily because you conclude you can handle that with no trouble and with no health or behavioral consequences. However, that amount could be grossly too much for your 120 lb. wife.

The typical alcoholic tries to control his drinking, fails to do so, and tries again and again. Eventually, those who are lucky decide to stop drinking altogether. There are various sources of help for this, including medical assistance, but the most beneficial social help is Alcoholics Anonymous.

The famous organization Alcoholics Anonymous started out with just two alcoholics trying to help each other. The principle of the self-help groups is that you ally yourself with one or more people who have your problem and you help each other in a variety of ways. (See Chapter 32.)

Some years ago a new self-help group appeared, consisting of people who felt that the Alcoholics Anonymous program was not really applicable to them because they could not identify themselves as alcoholics, nor did they feel the need to adhere to the major AA principle of total abstention. The new group was called "Drinkwatchers." Chapters of this organization have appeared in various parts of the country. Another group publishes a newsletter known as *Responsible Drinkers*. Information about these and other sources of help is listed in Chapter 34.

Abstainers can be happy

If the thought of life without alcohol seems overwhelmingly depressing, go to an open meeting of your local Alcoholics Anonymous group. There you will see the happy faces of people who have learned to live very full and satisfactory lives without alcoholic beverages of any kind. I will say more about AA in later Chapters, but note that you do not have to identify yourself as "an alcoholic" to go to one of their open meetings. You can go along merely as an interested citizen or someone who wants to see what it is all about. Indeed, there are certain groups of people, such as ministers, nurses, and doctors who should make a point of going to an AA meeting simply as part of their professional education.

Summary

In this chapter, I have asked you to look at your past drinking behavior, to consider the facts as they have been presented, and to make an honest appraisal of your drinking. If you are not ready to do that, I have suggested that you keep a diary of your drinking for the next few months to help in making the appraisal. Your informed decision may be to continue as an abstainer, to continue as a moderate drinker, to reduce a slightly hazardous level of drinking or a significantly dangerous one, to try to maintain a more reasonable level of drinking, or to stop altogether.

Current statistics indicate that excessive drinkers are exposed to a large variety of health hazards and accident risks. Being an alcoholic and doing nothing about your drinking means that on an average you will sacrifice between ten and twelve years of your life. Ask yourself this question: "Is my excessive drinking worth the probability of dying ten to twelve years prematurely?"

WHAT

SPECIAL

PEOPLE

WANT TO KNOW

chapter sixteen

Children

and

Drinking

This chapter is addressed especially to children—particularly to preteenagers. However, since we have all been children, every reader can benefit from reading this chapter.

I hope that you have read or will read Section One of this book, because you need to know the facts about alcohol. I was raised at a time and in a society when occasionally I would hear an adult say, in hushed tones, "He drinks!"—a statement that carried a message of horror, mystery, and criticism. Of course, it did not take me long to learn that the phrase meant that, "He drinks alcoholic beverages," and after a while I discovered that it really meant, "He drinks to excess, or alcoholically."

If adults in your home drink moderately and with no

evidence of troubles resulting from that drinking, then you are relatively lucky because you are being exposed to a good model. If these adults are your parents, you probably do not have a physical constitution that makes you more at risk to have trouble with alcohol than the average individual. Of course, if you are adopted, then you may not have the benefit of knowing.

There are laws regarding who can purchase alcoholic beverages, and these are relatively wise. However, there are no laws saying that it is illegal for an adult to give you a sip of their drink, and, if you are really interested and they are willing to do so, go ahead. The probability is that you will not enjoy the taste and may even wonder why on earth anyone would drink that awful stuff. As you grow older, however, probably your taste will change.

There have been times when drinking water was not safe, and children in such cultures were given wine or beer with their meals. Sometimes even in some of today's cultures, quite young children are given such drinks, sometimes diluted with water. I know of no evidence that this is particularly harmful, except that it introduces a poisonous substance at a stage when the body cells are still actively growing and multiplying. Alcohol does interfere with this growth, which is a good reason to advise avoidance of alcohol until growth is over.

Another important reason for children to avoid alcohol is because of its major effect on the liver. The liver is an organ in which a great deal of chemical activity goes on, including the storage of sugars in a special form that can be rapidly released when energy is needed. Children in an actively growing phase and with a lot of bodily activity can only store enough sugars to last for a few hours. That is probably why you feel hungry quite often. Unfortunately, alcohol interferes with the proper storage and release of these important energy substances. Thus, if someone in your age group drinks enough alcohol (even just a few ounces of spirits) to affect the performance of the liver, there may be a sudden drop in blood sugar. The brain depends on a constant supply of sugar in the blood for its operation, and if this drops too low a person can become unconscious. If the individual is not found and quickly taken to a hospital for treatment, they can remain in coma and die.

Every year, doctors in hospital emergency rooms see children who are brought in unconscious. Sometimes they will be found at home with an open bottle of sherry or whiskey, and sometimes from the smell on their breath people just assume that they have passed out from drinking. However, they have not passed out from the amount of alcohol they have consumed but from the fact that their blood sugar level has become critically low. Unless properly treated in a medical setting, they may die or suffer permanent brain injury.

Knowing these facts makes it fairly clear that drinking-age laws have a basis for justification. On the other hand, there is no harm in your taking a sip or two of an adult's drink in order to see what it is like, particularly if it is while you are eating a meal.

"Growing up" is an important future consideration for all children, even though it sometimes seems so far away. Sometimes children want to play at being grown up by imitating older people. Because older people are often seen to be smoking cigarettes, sometimes young children pretend to be smoking with the aid of candy cigarettes. Starting real smoking is often a way whereby a child or a teenager tries to act "grown up." Unfortunately, this is a dangerous way of copying adults, since smoking is a risky activity. In this book we are concerned with drinking, which also is a way of acting grown up: it, too, is risky. There are lots of better ways of showing that you are mature. These include showing mature behavior in your habits, such as studying conscientiously, not wasting time on stupid television shows, being able to fend for yourself, and showing peers and adults that you can be trusted with responsibility. Belonging to a group such as the Boy Scouts or Girl Scouts can be a useful way of learning skills that will serve you in asserting your independence and your maturity.

When you eventually make the decision "to drink or not to drink" I hope that it will be based on understanding the facts and not on needing to use the process of drinking as a means of imitating grownups.

If you know classmates who boast about drinking alcohol and perhaps even bring alcohol to school or come to school "stoned" you should feel sorry for them, not envious. Some of them feel very childish and are trying to hide this by their "grownup behavior." Others have serious psychological problems that should be taken to a counselor for help. Anyone who is drinking to escape from such problems is doomed to failure. A more mature approach would be to talk problems over with parents, teacher, doctor, minister, school counselor, scout leader, or some other person whom you respect. Some child drinkers are already "hooked" on alcohol: they have developed tolerance and suffer the pangs of withdrawal when they stop. Such an individual requires outside help and probably medical attention, perhaps even hospitalization.

If you live in a family in which there are adults who drink to excess or show the alcoholic drinking patterns that I have described in this book, then I have some important things to say to you. First, if one or both of your parents are showing signs of alcoholism, take it as a warning that you, too, probably are carrying some physical predisposition to have trouble with alcohol if you choose to drink. Anyone with this history who can avoid starting to drink may be doing a great deal to protect himself or herself. Second, try to realize and understand that you are not the cause of your parent's heavy drinking, even though your father or mother may at times try to lay the blame on you. Some mothers who are alcoholics will try to find excuses for their drinking by saying, for example, that of course they had to drink a bottle of sherry because of all the noise the kids were making. Fathers may come home intoxicated saying that this is because they are worried about the cost of raising a family. Clearly things like this are pure excuses, and it is important for you not to feel blameworthy or guilty.

You also must understand that just as you did not make your parent become an alcoholic, neither can you stop them from being alcoholic. You can encourage them to know all that they can about alcohol and alcoholism, for instance, by reading a book like this one. Perhaps, also, there may be some trusted adult to whom you can talk about the drinking problems in the family. This could be an adult relative, minister, your family doctor, or a school counselor.

If there is alcoholism in your family and you are still a preteenager, one thing you can do is to start associating with people who have the same problem. Read the information in this book about Alcoholics Anonymous and about the program known as Al-Anon, which was developed for the husbands, wives and friends of alcoholics (Chapter 32). Now we are beginning to see the development of Al-Anon family groups, and in some areas teenagers have set up Alateen groups that I will talk about in the chapter addressed to teenagers. Even younger groups, nicknamed "Al-Atots," are starting in some areas to provide information to people who are still in their preteens and who have alcoholism in the home.

Remember, no matter what they tell you or imply to you, you did not and could not make your mother or father become an alcoholic!

chapter seventeen

Teenagers

and

Drinking

All teenagers and many others who were once teenagers should read this chapter. If you are a teenager, you should also look back at the previous chapter.

In the United States today, about 40 percent of children have a least tasted alcohol by the age of 10, and the average age at which most people take their first drink is between 12 and 13. The National Institute on Alcohol Abuse and Alcoholism estimates that in this country, among junior high and high school students, over three million students have drinking problems such as school and learning difficulties, emotional problems, problems with the law, and so on.

Drinking is a form of "rite of passage," whereby one expresses one's adulthood. But there is a big difference between learning to drink for pleasure, a mild high, and some relaxation, and drinking to a state of stupefaction. Also, there are correct and incorrect times and places to drink.

If you are drinking in school, you are impairing your capacity to learn. Even if, while drinking, you are maintaining honor grades, the fact is that you could be doing even better without drinking. You may say that you are so bored in school that you have to drink to survive. If this is true, and not just an excuse, then you should be talking with your school counselor about getting into a special program that will be more challenging. Feel free to tell the counselor that you go to class "high" or "stoned" as this no longer shocks a trained and knowledgeable adult. You need help to assist you in getting out of such a pattern.

Everything I have said about family alcoholism in the previous chapter applies to you. If there is alcoholism in your family, be warned that you are more at risk for alcoholism. Indeed, under these circumstances you should immediately seek out an Alateen group to belong to. This is true whether or not you are already drinking.

If you are drinking heavily, whether at school, in the evenings, or on weekends, then consider all the information provided in this book and try to decide what would be a more realistic level for you to achieve. Make an informed decision about your drinking and see if you can adhere to that decision as described in Chapter 15.

Please remember that you have grown up being exposed to an enormous number of subtle adult influences that you knew nothing about. You have watched television for thousands of hours and you have become totally saturated with the message that for every problem there is a concrete solution. I am not exaggerating when I say that you have been exposed to years of brainwashing that has told you again and again that there is something you can take or do to overcome unhappiness and interpersonal problems. Television advertising has pounded into your head the concept that an unhappy boy or girl needs some expensive and complex new toy; a person with a pounding headache simply needs to swallow the correct pill; the person with bad breath (and, consequently, poor relationships with the opposite sex) simply needs to use the correct mouth-wash or toothpaste. You have been conditioned from early life on to believe that you have a right to instant and even continuous happiness, and that in the absence of this, all you have to do is put something in your mouth and swallow it. This attitude, I believe, is a significant factor in the drug and alcohol culture that you live in. Of course, there are other factors, and this book discusses many of them, for example, the concept that alcohol is "the adult drug," and that by using it you are expressing your adulthood. I have even heard parents say such things as, "Thank Goodness Billy is just drinking and not using drugs." Such a parental attitude is likely to be expressed by an adult with considerable ignorance about alcohol who is, of course, an alcohol user himself.

Keep in mind that alcohol impairs whatever you are doing, however slightly, and that the impairment is dose-related. That means that the more you drink, the more impairment there will be. The more recently learned any skill is, the more likely it is to be affected by drinking. The sad fact is that automobile accidents are the most common cause of death among teen-agers and young adults. At this age, there is a tendency to want to show off to others as a means of expressing one's maturity and adulthood. Risk taking also tends to appeal to young adults, and alcohol, as well as other drugs, greatly increases the tendency to take risks. To a considerable extent, there is a sex bias in this area, with boys more likely to want to show off their driving skills than girls. The classic and tragic pattern involves a male teenager, recently licensed to drive and perhaps a quite skilled driver under normal circumstances. However, on this occasion he has other teenagers in the car with him, and thus he is more likely to show off. In addition, he, along with the others, has been drinking: not infrequently, they are drinking as they drive. With or without encouragement from the passengers, our drinking teenager or young adult driver begins to take risks because he wants to demonstrate his prowess and alcohol is impairing his judgement. The final misjudgement of his life is when he goes around a curve too fast, goes off the road, and hits a tree, often taking the lives of his passengers with him. Sometimes, of course, the drinking driver hits another car, and sometimes he is alone when he has that single car fatality that brings everything to a full stop.

The National Highway Traffic Administration reports that in 1977 there were over 4,000 fatalities involving drunken drivers under 20 years of age.

The fact is that if you combine a recently acquired skill, such as driving, with another recently acquired skill, that of drinking, the combination creates a severe hazard. Please note that this is not the same as saying that all, even light, drinking is incompatible with safe driving. For more about driving and drinking, see Chapter 29.

Another chapter that may be of special interest to you is Chapter 30, on sex and drinking. Also, please pay particular attention to Chapter 15, on the subject of making an informed decision about your drinking. You do not have to imitate the excessive drinking of your peers, and, if you are already having trouble with your drinking, this book suggests ways of avoiding trouble and ways of getting help.

chapter eighteen

Women

and

Drinking

Although this entire book is applicable to women and drinking, there are some special factors that should be underscored. Alcohol use and abuse have been shown to be related to social, psychological, and constitutional factors, as well as to the availability and price of alcohol. In this century we have seen significant attitudinal changes in society about what women can and should do. For example, during and after World War II it gradually became more acceptable for women to smoke cigarettes. Now they have the questionable distinction of catching up with men on lung cancer rates. In a similar way, social attitudes have changed with regard to the drinking done by women. At one time, women were under less pressure to drink: it was less expected of them. Of course, in those days, as at present, there were plenty of secret women drinkers. But now, women can drink in bars and cocktail lounges without anyone applying any moral judgement.

Alcohol availability is also a factor, because in many states the housewife can pick up table wine and fortified wine when she goes to the supermarket. Relative to the general cost of food, the cost of alcoholic beverages has been stable or even going down.

In the first section of this book I presented evidence that alcohol is a substance that provides relief from inner conflicts. Some of these conflicts are concerned with difficulties in expressing one's feelings or in feeling at ease with one's sexuality. Some studies indicate that many women who have trouble with alcohol appear to have conflicts about themselves in their role as women. Also, and perhaps this is a result of their heavy drinking, they tend to have a history of spontaneous abortions, failure to get pregnant, and gynecological symptoms.

One factor that must be considered with regard to drinking by women is the variation in hormone levels that occurs in cycles throughout the reproductive life. Although men also have variations in hormone levels, the changes occurring in women are more extreme and more likely to produce alterations in response to alcoholic beverages. This matter has only recently begun to be studied. For example, Dr. Ben Morgan Jones, the Director of the New York Research Institute on Alcoholism in Buffalo, has shown that the effects of alcohol vary according to the phase of the menstrual cycle. Given the same dose of alcohol, based on body weight, the blood alcohol levels reached are higher in women tested immediately before the onset of menstrual flow. The blood alcohol levels are lowest while menstruation is actually going on. Contraceptive pills introduce additional hormones into the body, and these, too, can influence a woman's susceptibility to alcohol. Indeed, some women find that they enjoy drinking less when taking the pill.

All women must know about the fetal alcohol syndrome. The association of drinking during pregnancy with birth defects appeared in the medical literature over many years and has recently been "rediscovered" and renamed the *fetal alcohol syndrome* (FAS). At the moment no one can claim that we know all that we need to. In the case of human pregnancies, research is difficult: thus, various researchers are carrying out studies of FAS in animals. For example, Dr. Fred Ellis at the University of North Carolina has developed an FAS animal model in beagle dogs. When he gives pregnant beagles alcohol in significant amounts (equivalent to a woman drinking over a pint a day of spirits), the pregnancies do not go to full term. At lower levels of drinking, the puppies born are smaller than normal and show facial deformities not unlike those described in human children with FAS.

From what we know about growing tissue, it seems highly probable that sensitivity to alcohol use by the mother is greatest during the early phases of the pregnancy. Therefore, a woman who is trying to get pregnant and who is still drinking cannot afford to wait until she knows she is pregnant before she stops drinking. By the time she has missed her first menstrual period, she has been pregnant for several days at the very least; the growing mass of cells that will become her baby is in a very critical stage of development and must be presumed to be at its most sensitive to toxic chemicals, including alcohol. Thus, the best advice for a woman who is trying to get pregnant is for her not to drink at all. If there are occasions where she feels she must take a drink, it would be wise to restrict this very severely to perhaps a glass of wine sipped while eating.

We still don't know enough about how the critical stages of development of the fetus are affected by the mother's drinking. The brain may be the organ most affected by alcohol in the tissues during the last three months of the pregnancy. This is the time of the brain's most rapid growth. Thus, even if a woman is drinking heavily into the first weeks or months of her pregnancy, there is still time for benefits to occur if she stops drinking. I talked recently about this with Dr. Henry Rosett of Boston University School of Medicine, who is an expert on the identification and prevention of FAS. He has compared mothers who continued to drink heavily throughout the pregnancy with mothers who reduced their heavy drinking before the last three months of pregnancy. In all instances, the mothers who stopped drinking had heavier and longer babies with more normal head size. Those who continued to drink heavily throughout the pregnancy did not all have obviously abnormal babies, but they had significantly more babies with impaired growth, including small head size, which reflects less growth of the brain. Thus, Dr. Rossett and colleagues have demonstrated that a pregnant woman who reduces her alcohol consumption during pregnancy will benefit her baby.

Nature sometimes seems to try to help, and occasionally I have come across women who report completely losing any appetite for alcohol during early pregnancy. They are lucky. If you are a woman who wishes to get pregnant and you cannot stop drinking, then you would be wise to seek help as described in Chapters 26, 32 and 34. Then, and only then, should you attempt a pregnancy.

If there is a relatively safe amount of alcohol consumption that a woman can take during various phases of pregnancy, it is not yet known, and therefore total abstinence is preferable.

Sometimes during the last weeks of a pregnancy, physicians will use alcohol to stop the onset of premature labor. Where there are medical indications for this, it seems justified. By that time the growing fetus is probably less susceptible to the effects of the alcohol, and the benefits of maintaining the pregnancy longer may outweigh the toxicity of the alcohol.

What are the features of fetal alcohol syndrome? It is believed that the full fetal alcohol syndrome is seen in about 1 percent of infant births to alcoholic women. The full FAS involves a small baby with a small head, mental retardation, a peculiar facial appearance, and possibly other deformities such as additional or missing fingers and toes, and heart defects. The mental retardation is irreversible, and older children with FAS have been described as showing hyperactivity and behavior problems in school. The facial appearance includes a protruding forehead, narrow rather slit-like eye openings, a thin upper lip that some people describe as giving a fishlike appearance to the mouth, a receding chin, deformed ears, and a short upturned nose.

FAS is by no means the only cause of fetal growth disorders giving rise to abnormal babies; there are also many other causes of mental retardation.

Minor varieties of FAS may not even be recognized by the obstetrician or pediatrician and, unfortunately, some of these medical specialists do not discuss alcohol intake with their pregnant patients. Just how much alcohol consumption is "safe" from the point of view of the developing baby is really unknown at this time. Thus, in mid-1977, when some publicity was given to FAS, the National Institute on Alcohol Abuse and Alcoholism recommended that pregnant women limit their drinking to two drinks of hard liquor per day, whereas the National Council on Alcoholism pointed out, more wisely in my opinion, that total avoidance of alcohol was the preferred way to go.

As I have already indicated, it is likely that susceptibility to damage by alcohol is greater during the early stages of pregnancy, but we simply do not know enough at this time to correlate stages of pregnancy, amount drunk, and certainty of FAS. Some experts believe that drinking as much as 10 or more ounces of hard liquor per day will bring about a risk of FAS as high as three out of four births. Remember, too, that equivalent amounts of wine and beer contain alcohol that is just as damaging.

Every time you take a drink, your unborn baby has one too! If you become drunk, then undoubtedly your unborn baby also becomes drunk. Dr. James Rose of the Bowman Gray School of Medicine has been studying alcohol in pregnant sheep and finds that the growing fetus of a ewe that is given alcohol retains the alcohol in its body longer than the mother and at higher levels.

What does all this mean for you, the woman drinker who is reading this? First of all, if you want to get pregnant, can you stop drinking altogether? If you can do so without difficulty, then your baby will certainly not be exposed to the dangers of FAS. If you cannot do so without difficulty, then you are already having problems with alcohol and may indeed be suffering from alcoholism. Under these circumstances, you should avoid getting pregnant until your alcoholism is well under control. Many chapters of this book provide suggestions about how to start working on this; one of the first things you must do is to face the facts, accept the truth, and decide to seek help. If you feel that continued heavy drinking is essential to you for the foreseeable future, then at least take absolute precautions to avoid pregnancy.

If you are of childbearing age and want to know more about the subject of alcohol and other drugs during pregnancy, consider reading the excellent book by Lucy Barry Robe that is listed in Chapter 34 of this book. You should also read Chapter 30 on Sex and Drinking.

chapter nineteen

Men

and Drinking

Drinking and heavy drinking have been associated with the macho masculine image for a long time. Indeed, at some times and in some cultures drinking has been the prerogative of men. In the chapter on teenagers, I pointed out that starting to drink is one of the ways whereby young people assert their desire to grow up. There are, however, better and safer ways of claiming one's maturity.

This chapter is particularly addressed to men, but is only meaningful if you have read Section One of this book in its entirety, because I will not repeat many of the important facts previously discussed.

Do recognize the fact that different people have different capacities for drinking. I have already explained why it is not reasonable or fair to expect women to drink as much as men. Similarly, a large man can drink more than a small man because the alcohol is diluted by the total water content of the body. In addition to this factor, there are individual differences in susceptibility. If you can boast that you have "a hollow leg," realize that this may be more of a liability than an asset. It may simply mean that the sensitive tissues of your body, such as the liver, are being bathed in alcohol for longer periods of time than they would be if you felt more affected by the alcohol and therefore stopped drinking earlier.

If you are sensitive to alcohol and cannot drink very much without discomfort or sleepiness, consider yourself as lucky in that regard.

In addition to recognizing the different capacities of individuals for alcoholic beverages, watch for changes in your own capacity. For example, as you get older, your capacity for alcohol will probably diminish. Likewise, various illnesses can change your ability to drink. Assuming that you are a drinker and, at the moment, a moderate one, keep watching how much you are drinking and watch for the warning signs of drinking too much. In particular, try to avoid situations in which there is a large or small group decision to get intoxicated. Having a few drinks with your friends or colleagues on Friday afternoon is a far different thing from saying, "Let's go and get smashed." Unfortunately, there still are groups of people, usually exclusively masculine, who set out with this express purpose. To do so is to accept a whole variety of risks.

One drinking situation that men seem to find themselves in much more than women is that of "ordering rounds." At such times, each man seems to feel honor bound to buy a round of drinks for everyone else. This, of course, leads to excessive drinking, if the group contains more than three or four people. If you find yourself in the midst of a round-buying situation, insist on being one of the early ones to buy for everyone else. Explain, if you need to, that you are going to have to leave early, but want to treat your buddies before you go. That way you can uphold your honor and still do only a moderate amount of drinking in spite of peer group pressure. If you find yourself in a larger group, there are various strategies you can follow. Under these circumstances, as always, make a decision in advance as to how much you are going to drink and over what period of time. Thus, you might make it clear to your drinking buddies that you will have to leave in one and a half hours, for example. If you don't wish to leave, but wish to drink less, feel free to order a soft drink on every second round. It is better to have your acquaintances (I won't call them friends) needle you about this than to have to struggle home in a stupefied state and suffer a hangover the next day. If you feel that you need to explain why you are drinking less, say that you are doing it for health reasons or because you are training for a marathon, or because your doctor is planning some tests, or whatever. The average heavy drinker will get off your back under such circumstances and probably will not remember anything about it later, anyway.

May you continue to drink in good health!

chapter twenty

Minorities

and

Drinking

Since the average North American today is of white Anglo-Saxon stock, this chapter in particular is for the attention of Afro-Americans, American Indians, Chicanos, Oriental Americans, and all others who do not identify themselves as being largely of European origin.

In the first place, do understand that there are built-in racial differences in response to drugs just as there are certain diseases associated more with one race than with another. Thus, if you find that alcohol seems to have peculiar effects on you, this may represent some inborn characteristic that you can do nothing about. I have already described the alcohol sensitivity found in many Oriental people. Those who find their reaction to alcohol generally uncomfortable should look upon themselves as lucky, because they will have a hard time drinking enough to become truly dependent on alcohol. I believe that there is probably a similar sensitivity among some Jewish people, although, in my experience, it more often is presented as digestive upsets and pains following alcohol intake. Again, this can be an asset because it seems to provide a protection.

The situation regarding American Indians is somewhat confused at present. One of the earlier studies comparing the rate of the breakdown of alcohol between Indians and Canadians of European origin showed that Indians and Eskimos in Alberta reached higher blood levels of alcohol and kept these longer. The implication was that perhaps this physiological difference could explain why Indians have more trouble with alcohol. However, there have been other studies in both the United States and Canada that produced different results. A major problem is that we cannot simply assume that all American Indians are alike metabolically. This subject is still under research and eventually we will know whether or not inborn physiological factors cause all or some Indians to be more at risk to have trouble with alcohol if they drink. The fact that there are high rates of drinking and problems with alcohol among Indians appears to be well established, although there are some anthropologists who dispute it.

On a historical scale, it appears that the vast majority of Indians who were roaming the North American continent before the arrival of Europeans did not have alcohol. They tended to be nomadic in many cases, and in some instances they had discovered mind-altering drugs in the form of plants such as certain cactuses. It may be that some of the Atlantic Seaboard Indians were acquainted with fermented grape juice, since grapes were native to that area, according to early reports of white settlers. It appears that the natives of Central America also made alcoholic beverages before the arrival of Europeans. These, probably, were used in a variety of religious and tribal ceremonies, and there were severe penalties for getting drunk at the wrong time and place.

The overall conclusion that is forced on us is that North American Indians had little or no exposure to alcohol before the arrival of Europeans. Some fascinating historical research on the topic of "fire water" and Indians is described in the book *Drunken Comportment,* by MacAndrew and Edgerton.

From the racial point of view, we can say that North American Indians have had significantly less time than those of European origin to "learn" to deal with alcohol. By the word *learning* I refer to both the development of cultural attitudes toward this potent substance and the possibility that repeated exposure to alcohol by succeeding generations may lead to some selective breeding advantageous to future generations. It might be, for example, that those Europeans who were most prone to have trouble with alcohol were also liable to breed less effectively, thus passing less predisposition for alcoholism down through the generations. Any race such as the North American Indians that has only been exposed to alcohol for a relatively short period of time would not yet have begun to show the effects of selective breeding.

In considering the issue of minorities and drinking, there is also the question of cultural patterns and environment. Some cultures seem to recommend, and even require, heavy drinking as a means of demonstrating strength and prowess. The "macho" image that is particularly identified with Central and South American cultures is one example.

Drinking by blacks in the United States appears to be lower than that of whites, particularly among women. On the other hand, the immoderate use of alcohol, problem drinking, and alcoholism do not spare the blacks. One unfortunate fact is that blacks appear to be more susceptible than whites to liver damage from the use of alcohol.

From the point of view of the environment, we must consider the fact that alcohol provides escape, however temporary. For those minorities who live in poor housing, who are economically disadvantaged, perhaps culturally deprived, and suffering from excessive unemployment, alcohol can provide a tempting escape from harsh and bitter reality. In the ghettos of our large cities and on Indian reservations, a high percentage of people suffer from an attitude of hopelessness, low opportunity, thwarted ambition, and loss of optimism. Such circumstances must contribute to the high rate of suicide among young females and the high rate of alcoholism among males.

It would be quixotic for us to assume that we could wipe out alcoholism among minorities merely by improving social, educational, and cultural opportunities. I have shown throughout this book that we can only understand this disease if we take into account alcohol availability (including cost,) sociocultural factors, and biomedical factors. Sociocultural improvements cannot by themselves be expected to wipe out alcoholism. However, such improvements are not only owed to our minority citizens, but are also bound to produce some beneficial effects with regard to drinking and drinking to excess.

chapter twenty-one

Drinking

and

Special Risk

Groups

Who is at special risk to have trouble if they drink? I have
already made it clear that any human being who drinks is
taking a risk, however acceptable that may be. However, there
are some special segments of the population that deserve
special mention.

Physicians

Physicians and other health professionals appear to be at
higher risk for problems with alcohol than the general population. For one thing, more of them drink. For another, they

tend to be ambitious, driven people who could be described as "hard working and hard playing."

I have met more than a few physicians who are now ready to admit that they were drinking to excess while medical students. These are the ones who are usually recognized as heavy drinkers by their classmates. Drinking heavily while serving the long hours of a house officer or intern is not easy, but some such individuals hit the bottle whenever they go off duty thereby drinking themselves into a restless sleep. Residents in training in various specialties also have their fair share, and perhaps a bit more, of alcohol problems.

In addition to those with early signs of alcoholism (perhaps this is "primary" alcoholism, in most cases) we find those whose drinking problems begin after they have gotten themselves established. Once the long and arduous medical and specialty training is over, the doctor can begin to reap the rewards as he finds himself in a position of high responsibility, high tension, and high pressure. By now he has the resources with which to surround himself with worldly comforts, one of which is a liberal supply of alcohol.

At this point in his career, he may start to rely significantly upon alcohol for relaxation and "getting away from it all." Perhaps he begins to experience a feeling of letdown or disappointment in his career choice or in his degree of success. Once again, alcohol can supply the escape. His busy life and major responsibilities may even interfere with his duties as a father and husband. Difficulties in these areas can also lead to his reaching for a drink.

Everything I have said so far has implied that we are talking about male physicians, but female physicians are just as liable to develop problems with alcohol. Likewise, other health professionals appear to be more at risk, including dentists, nurses, and paramedical professionals. The tradition of "hard working, hard playing, and hard drinking" is undoubtedly a factor. In one of our student surveys of health professionals we found 95 percent of them using alcohol, which is far in excess of the overall general population. There may be other subtle factors that have not been studied sufficiently as yet. It seems to me that people who have had training in understanding and dealing with drugs sometimes develop a sort of contempt for the laws of pharmacology (the science that studies the actions of drugs). Certainly, when a nurse or doctor first gives himself a dose of a potent drug such as morphine, he appears to do so while maintaining a mental attitude of, "Just this one time won't hurt me; addiction can't happen to me. I know enough about these things to avoid being trapped." Of course, none of these assertions is true.

Similar thinking can influence the health professional when it comes to the use and overuse of alcohol. Indeed, it contributes, I believe, to the difficulty that many doctors have in recognizing alcoholism in their patients. After all, if the physician is drinking regularly (and with perhaps some self-doubt or guilt), he is bound to find it more difficult to recognize the patient who is drinking alcoholically. In some of my presentations to doctors I have said in jest, but not without truth, that doctors have trouble recognizing alcoholism unless the patient clearly drinks more than the doctor!

One of my psychiatrist friends was required to go to an Alcoholics Anonymous meeting as part of his training in psychiatry. He describes how they went over a questionnaire about drinking. If you answered more than two or three with a *yes*, you were having trouble with alcohol. He answered more than half of the questions *yes* (secretly to himself), and concluded that this was a bunch of zealots who were down on any drinking. After many more years of drinking, the breakup of his marriage, the loss of professional status, and a visit to a state hospital, he was finally able to recognize that he suffered from alcoholism and needed to be a member of AA.

In North America today there is an organization known as International Doctors in Alcoholics Anonymous. They already have nearly 2,000 members, and it is clear that thousands more need to join.

For a long time the medical profession has acted very irresponsibly with regard to its own impaired colleagues; whether impaired by mental illness, drug addiction, or alcoholism. The tendency was to try to cover up for the incompetency of their colleague, which, in the long run, was doing him no favor. Today, fortunately, we are seeing a more responsible attitude. Medical societies have special procedures for identifying the alcoholic physician, confronting him with the evidence of his illness, and helping him to get into a treatment program. Over the years I have treated more physician alcoholics and drug addicts than any other single occupational class. It has been my experience that they respond well to a treatment program once their denial of illness has been overcome, usually because of coercion and pressure from colleagues, family, hospital authorities, or medical licensing boards. It has been calculated that in the United States annually we lose the equivalent of one entire class of graduating medical students by death, retirement, and loss of license due to alcoholism and drug addiction. Here, then, is a group of people who deserve identification and compassionate help, since they can then return to the important health care functions for which they were trained.

Everything I have said above applies equally to the alcoholic pharmacist, optometrist, podiatrist, dentist, nurse, or any other health professional. For that matter, it applies to the alcoholic judge, professor, attorney, clergyman, or business person.

Priests and nuns

The available statistics indicate that those men and women who serve in the Roman Catholic Church are probably a special high risk group for alcoholism. Needless to say, for a long time there has been a tendency to brush the facts under the rug, but recently some more honest reports have been published.

There may well be a constitutional predisposition for alcoholism in some people who become priests or nuns, particularly if their heritage goes back to Ireland. I have no proof of this at present but feel sufficiently certain to put this speculation in writing.

Those who choose the celibate life of devotion to religion must possess certain specific personality characteristics and perhaps even some special psychological conflicts. Because of its use in religious ceremonies, they have easy access to wine;

this, and not just the small amount actually used at Mass, puts them at risk. Some priests and nuns have reported feeling tremendous personality changes when they drank enough wine and that they returned to it again and again as a favorite escape or coping mechanism. With easy access to large volumes of alcohol, such people can soon be drinking enough to become tolerant and to show a withdrawal syndrome if their supplies are stopped.

What is called for is a change in attitude very much like that required for the alcoholic health professional. We must no longer think of it as "inconceivable" that a priest or nun could be an alcoholic. Indeed, we should think of it as a probability any time that a priest or nun is found to be having significant emotional and interpersonal problems. Once again, bringing the possibility out into the open enables the involved individual to begin to be more honest with himself and others and introduces the opportunity for a planned rehabilitation program.

Creative and artistic people

Ernest Hemingway said that most good writers are alcoholic. In 1970 Dr. Donald Goodwin recorded that of seven Americans so far awarded the Nobel Prize for Literature, four were alcoholics and a fifth drank heavily. He concluded that in a list of well-known American writers of the past century, between one-third and one-half could be considered alcoholic.

In Chapter 34 you will find listed three articles by Dr. Goodwin on the alcoholism of Eugene O'Neill, F. Scott Fitzgerald, and Georges Simenon. In O'Neill's case, he usually either drank *or* wrote, but did not mix the two. To begin with, Fitzgerald followed a similar pattern, but in his early thirties he began to drink while working. Once he wrote, "A short story can be written on a bottle, but for a novel you need the mental speed that enables you to keep the whole pattern in your head." He struggled throughout his life with attempts to control his drinking, staying dry for months, but inevitably relapsing. Alcohol was the "writer's vice," he rationalized, claiming that it "heightened feeling." In Simenon's case he believed that alcohol would kill him, but that he could not write without it. Eventually it turned out that he could, since neither the quantity nor the quality of his work suffered when he was abstinent.

In a 1973 paper, Goodwin writes, "Despite the 'charms of drunkenness', most writers are not drunkards. In America, it just *seems* that most writers are drunkards. This is because so many of them have been famous and visible."

I do not have any reliable statistics on alcohol use or abuse by creative and artistic people. However, I think that such people do need a few paragraphs of commentary.

Keep in mind that if you feel your creativity "requires" the use of alcohol, you are immediately putting yourself more at risk to have problems with alcohol or alcoholism. If you believe that alcohol permits you to get in closer touch with your "inner self," try finding less toxic ways of doing so. Perhaps you can accomplish this by planned relaxation, meditation, running, or even just by remembering and recording your dreams. Whatever you do, try to use alcohol in a recreational context rather than a creational one. If you depend upon alcohol to "unleash your creativity," then undoubtedly, unless you are willing to accept a very low productivity, you are going to be exposed to unacceptably high levels of alcohol.

Creative and artistic people tend to be more self aware and sensitive than most, but there is no evidence that alcohol provides significant or beneficial enhancement of this quality or that it is a safe or reliable cure for such problems as writer's block.

Bartenders and drinking

Of course, not all bartenders drink, but those that do appear to be somewhat at risk for problems. In this instance, the issue is one of availability and low or absent cost. If this is coupled with other factors (psychological problems or family history) predisposing toward alcoholism, then we have a bad combination. Everything in this book applies to bartenders, and they should particularly pay attention to the questionnaires for identifying alcoholism, the tips for safer drinking, and the techniques for self-monitoring.

Housepainters and drinking

On many occasions I have heard alcoholics claim that housepainters are a special risk group and I have heard housepainters make the same assertion. I have no statistics for this, nor do I know of anyone who has. Undoubtedly, house-painters are exposed to fumes of substances that, once absorbed into the body, must be destroyed by the liver. Whether or not there is any correlation between this and excessive alcohol use I do not know. Some housepainters with whom I have discussed this question assert that they drink alcohol to help them cope with the smell and taste of the substances they use in their work. This sounds like the usual search for rationalization on the part of the heavy drinker. Surely, soft drinks would do just as well.

It may be, of course, that people who are already alcoholic, or significantly predisposed to become so, drift into the occupation of housepainting. Some occupations may contribute to a need to seek alcohol escape by being boring and personally unrewarding.

Business executives and drinking

As the executive moves higher and higher up the business ladder, he or she tends to have more money to spend and thus is more likely to purchase alcoholic beverages. In addition, the executive probably has more and more social functions to attend for business reasons and these are likely to be associated with drinking. Finally, comes the stage in which he is left in relative isolation, with his own office, perhaps his own rest-room, and even his own bar. Many business executives are protected by loyal and well-meaning secretaries when they are sleeping off the effects of a three martini lunch or are sitting there unproductively on Monday morning trying to recover from a hangover. This protection and relative isolation are predisposing factors that encourage continued drinking and enhance the probability of alcoholism. The executive at the top no longer has the benefit of a superior who is "looking over his shoulder." These appear to be the reasons for executives getting into trouble with alcohol, and all people in business should be familiar with the facts in this book.

The executive who is put into an office with a built-in bar should consider never opening it during business hours, or, better still, never using it at all. Everything I have said and will say in this book about monitoring one's drinking needs to be carried out more carefully than ever when there are unlimited opportunities to drink.

Compared to the high-powered executive in his private suite, the blue-collar worker or the office worker with many fellow workers is at an advantage. At least during working hours, he or she is relatively protected from succumbing to the impulse to drink. If they do drink on the job, they are more likely to be spotted and confronted with the need to get help. The executive, on the other hand, when protected by his or her secretary, is being pushed into a more and more hazardous state. What should the secretary do under such circumstances? The answer depends upon the particular situation, but it might include speaking to the spouse of the executive, taking a much less "protective" role, and possibly even expressing concern to the boss in terms of his or her health and business future. This is discussed further in Chapter 25.

Sales representatives and drinking

Much of what was said about the business executive applies to you if you are out on the road, making sales, and having social contacts with customers. It is easy to rationalize that your job "requires" you to drink. No job requires you to drink too much. Likewise, if you spend lonely nights in hotels or motels,

it is easy to convince yourself that there is nothing else to do but to drink.

Take inventory of yourself and your life situation. If you are drinking in a hazardous manner, can you stop? If not, perhaps you should give up your sales position. A job back in the home office might be much safer for you.

Some sales representatives have found it possible to occupy their evenings away from home in ways other than drinking to excess. In some cities there are excellent cultural opportunities to be enjoyed in the evenings. However, this is rarely true in small town America, and other solutions must be found. Can you find a gym to go and take a workout? How about jogging or swimming? Could you take up an interesting hobby that calls for a clear mind that you could carry with you to your hotel room? Even a computer to play chess against you would soon pay for itself under these circumstances. Or perhaps you could learn to put together small electronic parts that could be easily carried in the trunk of your car, thus making your own radio or television set or computer.

If, as a salesman on the road, you spend many evenings with other salesmen drinking to excess, then it is up to you to find ways of avoiding this or of coping with it without drinking to excess yourself. If you choose to do nothing, at least realize that your health is at stake and that you are shortening your life.

Drinking and other special risk groups

No doubt there are other special occupational groups that I could focus upon, but the principles mentioned throughout this book apply in all cases. People with a family history of alcoholism constitute a special risk group, as do people with psychological difficulties for which alcohol gives relief. The same is true for lonely housewives, bored people, unhappy people, and so on. There are ways of getting out of the vicious cycle of drinking, excessive drinking, and alcoholism. Read on!

chapter twenty-two

Drinking

and

the Senior

Citizen

By the term *senior citizen* I refer particularly to those aged 65 and over who have retired from their regular occupation. Alcoholics live shorter lives than the general population, therefore significantly fewer alcoholics reach the status of senior citizen. The moderate, even though regular, use of alcohol is associated with slightly greater longevity. Thus, many, but not all, senior citizens have been used to moderate social drinking for many years. However, retirement often brings major changes in a person's way of life, and some of these changes increase the probability of having problems with alcohol.

Many people, as they get older, become increasingly susceptible to the less desirable effects of alcohol, such as digestive disturbances, sleep problems, and hangovers. If you find that you cannot comfortably drink as much as you used to, you should regard this as a blessing, since it offers you protection from overuse.

One danger of retirement is boredom, particularly if you have moved from familiar territory to a new area where perhaps you do not have the friends and acquaintances that were once available. The major problem, however, is often that of having too much time on one's hands. Drinking alcoholic beverages seem to help to pass the time, initially at least, but unfortunately it carries the hazards that this book is all about. Clearly, it is desirable to put alcohol into a secondary position in your lifestyle and to keep it there. This might involve resolving to do no more than a certain amount of drinking and only at certain times, such as the hour before dinner or the hour before going to bed.

If you were formerly married and are now living alone, you are probably more at risk than ever, since you no longer have a spouse to help to monitor your drinking and perhaps comment if you seem to be drinking too much. In particular, beware of drinking as a means of dampening down or even drowning out any sexual impulses you may have. Remember, too, that alcohol supplies calories, and that it is important during your senior years not to gain weight. An exercise program that is compatible with your health status should be undertaken regularly. If you have not been exercising, you should ask your personal physician to help you work out an exercise program.

Many older people say that they enjoy a "nightcap" before going to bed. If you feel that an alcoholic beverage contributes to your night's sleep and to your general well-being, it could well be so. However, if you are bothered with sleeplessness, fast beating heart during the night, or waking up too early, the alcohol could be the culprit. There is a tendency for the initial sedative effects of the alcohol to be followed by a reaction of increased activity.

Any time that you have unusual symptoms or feel sick, see your physician and be honest with him about your alcohol consumption. If he finds that alcohol is contributing to your disability, he will say so. If he finds that the alcohol is doing no harm, he will not object to your continuing to enjoy moderate drinking.

chapter twenty-three

Alcoholics

and Drinking

This chapter is aimed at those who are already alcoholics or who are beginning to suspect that they are alcoholics. For the latter, keep in mind that it is not really how much you drink (although obviously you can damage yourself with the poisonous effects of alcohol if you drink a lot), but what alcohol does to you in terms of physical and mental health, interpersonal relations, effect on family and friends, and overall functioning, including your work and your recreation. Chapter 35 provides a series of questionnaires that are helpful in identifying alcoholism by looking at the various traits of alcoholic drinking.

Now, assuming that you have either the knowledge or the strong suspicion that you suffer from alcoholism, let's see if we

114

can narrow it down further. I believe that our present knowledge permits us to conclude that there are two categories (at least) of alcoholics. From reading the earlier sections of this book, you may already have begun to classify yourself. Primary alcoholics are those who usually have a family history of alcohol problems, provided that there were drinkers in previous generations. It's possible that previous generations abstained from alcohol use on religious, moral, or social grounds, in which case, predisposed ancestors would have left no record of alcohol problems. However, if you know for sure that there were alcoholics among blood relatives in previous generations, or perhaps even among your brothers and sisters, then you must know immediately that you are more at risk to be a primary alcoholic.

Primary alcoholics are, in general, intelligent, personable, and pleasant people except when they are under the effects of excessive drinking. Usually they have no excess of the "neurotic" symptoms suffered by mankind in general such as anxiety, phobias, depression and so on. However, if they have been struggling for years with the knowledge that they have trouble in controlling their drinking, they may have a deep sense of frustration that can be very annoying. In addition, if they have been struggling with concern and guilt about their drinking behavior, they are likely to have deep feelings of insecurity, depression, remorse, loss of self-esteem and self-accusation. Primary alcoholics usually have little or no history of "normal drinking." In the very beginning their drinking differed from that of their friends and acquaintances. The first drink very often led to a kind of "breakthrough" experience, with perhaps the feeling that, "Now, for the very first time, I am alive," as one patient said to me. Primary alcoholics tend to get into trouble with alcohol relatively early in life, sometimes in their teens, often in their twenties, and almost always before the age of forty. When they stop drinking for days, weeks or months, which is very typical of their history, they eventually start drinking again and once again experience a "high," a relief of tension, and a sense of overall benefit. Unfortunately, for them it does not last. Once again, there is loss of control, drinking more than was intended, and, in general, an unhappy drinking experience. Frequently, this pattern is associated with a history of childhood problems that appeared in school before there was any drinking. Such problems include a history of being restless and having a poor attention span in class, with a tendency to be impulsive and to have problems in relation to teachers and other students. Such children often have had difficulty in handling their feelings, particularly those involving anger.

If the preceding description rings a bell in terms of describing you, then you should conclude that you are suffering from primary alcoholism. Such a conclusion is by no means all bad. It can be compared with the individual who is confronted with a diagnosis of diabetes: it simply means that some trait that you have inherited makes it impracticable for you to be a normal drinker. Frustrating though this may be, the realization that you are different from most other drinkers leaves you with the option of explaining this whenever you so choose, and with planning a lifestyle that eliminates alcohol, since, for you, its addictive and poisonous effects far exceed any advantages the drug effect may offer.

Once you have identified yourself as suffering from this condition, you need to start making plans regarding your lifestyle and the need to eliminate alcohol. If, to begin with, you find that being around drinkers is difficult, you may wish to avoid this. However, in the long run, you are going to have to be able to place yourself in drinking situations while not drinking yourself. Indeed, some of my friends who are recovering alcoholics tell me that going to cocktail parties is a reaffirmation of their intention not to drink. As one doctor put it, "It just takes one bad drunk at a party to help me to feel good about the fact that I am not drinking myself."

If your previous drinking buddies express surprise or dismay at your refusal of drinks, you have to learn to say something such as, "Sorry, fellows, I just can't drink right now, but don't let me stop you." If you want to give further explanations, you can use phrases such as, "Doctor's orders," or "I've got some medical tests coming up," or "I just can't handle it right now," or even "I am an alcoholic." The last statement should arouse respect, admiration, and understanding on the part of your friends. If they start protesting that you cannot be an alcoholic, then this may indicate that they, too, are having problems with alcohol. However, whether you identify yourself to any individual as an alcoholic or not depends upon the person, the circumstances, and the decisions that you have made for yourself.

When the organization Alcoholics Anonymous was first founded, there were greater and better reasons to claim anonymity and to maintain it than there are today. However, even today people should not identify themselves as members of Alcoholics Anonymous, even though they may choose to identify themselves as alcoholics or as "suffering from alcoholism." Alcoholism is less and less being perceived as a stigma, and if this book has accomplished anything, it has, I hope, indicated that anyone can suffer from alcoholism, and that this does not mean being weak willed, having a psychiatric disease, or being unreliable in other aspects of living.

If, as an alcoholic, you are attending Alcoholics Anonymous and have adopted their lifestyle, then you are to be congratulated and even envied. If, on the other hand, you are suffering from alcoholism and are not yet taking advantage of the benefits of belonging to Alcoholics Anonymous, then all I can do is to recommend your going to some meetings of that fine organization in order to see what you have been missing.

I do know several alcoholics who say that they went to a meeting and found that it consisted of a bunch of fanatics, or a bunch of unintelligent people, or even a bunch of eggheads. The point is that when choosing an Alcoholics Anonymous group you have to be just as careful as you would in choosing a church to join or finding the civic organization in which you would be comfortable. You need to be with people who match your style and your type of communication. There are groups that are attended mostly by blue-collar workers. Likewise, there are some whose members are mostly physicians, attorneys, and university professors. Clearly, the professor would find some difficulty in identifying with the blue-collar group, and vice-versa. The point is that you should shop around until you find a group in which you feel comfortable and at ease.

During the early weeks and months of sobriety, Alcoholics

Anonymous membership can be so important that for some people it can and should be attended many times a week. Some people even arrange their schedules so that they are at an AA meeting every night. This can be important in terms of constantly bolstering the resolution not to drink. However, as time goes by, a less total devotion to Alcoholics Anonymous can suffice. The alcoholics that I know find that regular attendance at AA meetings is a vital part of their lifestyle, without which they fear that they would relapse into drinking. One psychiatrist friend of mine who is a recovering alcoholic says that his AA membership is "both a burden and a salvation." He means that it takes time to go to meetings and that it is not always convenient, but he believes that not going to these meetings might begin a process of backsliding into the alcoholism that almost destroyed him years ago.

The great thing that Alcoholics Anonymous membership can give the alcoholic is a sense of comradeship and support and the knowledge that life can be enjoyable without drinking.

Throughout this book I have emphasized that there is a form of alcoholism that should be categorized "careless drinking." Alcoholics who fit this classification generally do not meet the criteria for primary alcoholics. They, too, can gain a great deal from membership in Alcoholics Anonymous. However, for some of them there *may* be an alternative. For example, the organization known as Responsible Drinkers is probably having its greatest success with secondary alcoholics, or "careless drinkers." This book, too, offers suggestions for monitoring one's drinking and for trying to bring it under control. Obviously, if you can succeed in doing this, and if you can make this your drinking style for the remainder of your life, then Alcoholics Anonymous membership and total abstinence may not be indicated for you. However, I do know of many instances of people who have had a series of episodes of thinking they had their drinking under control, finding that it went out of control again, and finally, in a state of anger, self-accusation and frustration, saying, "It would be easier to quit altogether than to go on this way." For such individuals, I believe that the earlier they decide to quit altogether and to become a total abstainer, the better.

From time to time you will read or hear of people who are allegedly training alcoholics to become "controlled" or "social" drinkers. Just a few years ago the "Rand Report" produced waves of consternation among many people, particularly those who adhere to the principles of Alcoholics Anonymous. That report was a follow-up study on clinics treating patients with alcoholism. The discovery was made, not surprisingly, that a small number of people, instead of becoming total abstainers, had reduced their drinking to the point that, for the time being, at least, it was no longer bothersome to themselves or others. Similar findings have come from numerous follow-up studies on groups of people who have been loosely called "alcoholics." I believe that the explanation is quite simple. In any group of 100 "alcoholics," most of the individuals will be primary alcoholics, but a few will be of the secondary variety whose careless drinking has been superimposed upon psychological problems, internal personality conflicts, anxieties, depression, and so on, possibly aided and abetted by social factors such as living in a group with a heavy drinking style. A certain number of such individuals with secondary alcoholism are bound to be able to become more responsible in their drinking habits if they monitor themselves and if there are appropriate reasons for cutting back their drinking, such as health concerns expressed by their physician, threats from their spouse or employer, or even the personal realization: "Drinking this much can't be good for me."

It is even possible to make an analogy in the case of the disease of diabetes. Some diabetics have the severe variety that calls for careful dietary control plus the daily use of insulin. These could be considered to be equivalent to our primary alcoholics. Others, however, usually obese and indulging in careless dieting, can bring their diabetes under control by becoming careful dieters and by losing weight. The second group is equivalent to our secondary alcoholics, who can sometimes replace careless drinking with responsible drinking. This is the goal of the Responsible Drinkers organization, but please note that that group makes no attempt to replace or supplant Alcoholics Anonymous. Alcoholics Anonymous is obviously the only sensible way to go for the primary alcoholic.

If, after reading this, you are still doubtful as to whether you are a primary or a secondary alcoholic, then you must follow the instructions in this book about monitoring your drinking and bringing it down to less risky levels. Can you do so, and can you do so indefinitely? If you can, and if you have not met the general description of the primary alcoholic, then you are probably a secondary alcoholic, and maybe you can enjoy the privilege of being a drinker for the rest of your life. Remember, though, that drinking is a privilege that carries the responsibility of not damaging yourself or others.

Various groups throughout North America are offering training to become controlled drinkers for alcoholics. If you are wondering whether you should expose yourself to such a plan, read on. Such an approach is based on the psychological concept that alcoholism is simply a behavioral disorder, that is, that it represents carelessness in one's style of drinking. Obviously, such a concept takes no notice of the evidence for biological factors such as I have presented in earlier sections of this book. Behavioral psychologists look at what animals or humans do in terms of rewards and punishments. Behavior that is rewarded tends to increase, whereas behavior that is punished tends to decrease. Thus, a variety of treatment programs have been developed with the objective of turning alcoholics back into "social drinkers" or "controlled drinkers." I think there is a difference between social drinkers and controlled drinkers, in the sense that social drinkers only drink when there are social occasions to do so, which might be relatively infrequently, such as at a party. On the other hand, I do believe that everyone who is a serious or regular drinker should be a controlled drinker in the sense that he or she has control of the amount, determines in advance how much to drink, does not exceed the planned quantity, does not show behavioral problems related to drinking, and, thus, does not show loss of control.

The first time that I heard of anyone trying to turn alcoholics into controlled drinkers was in 1970 when I attended a Congress on Alcoholism in Australia. There, I was fascinated by the report of two psychologists from Sydney, Professor Sid Lovibond and his graduate student Glen Caddy (the latter now Dr. Caddy at Old Dominion University, Norfolk, Virginia).

Lovibond and Caddy had decided to take a strictly behavioral approach to alcoholism and to train their patients to recognize their blood level while drinking in the treatment situation. Patients who exceeded the blood alcohol target were punished by electric shock, and this appeared to help them to develop a state of control.

I returned to the United States with considerable excitement regarding this approach. (Keep in mind that then the evidence for nurture over nature was still considerable, and that the important proof of an inborn factor for alcoholism had not yet been provided.) I already knew that most of my alcoholic patients were, initially at least, unhappy about the idea of becoming total abstainers. Quite naturally, they wished that they could go on drinking, but with control. I decided to try to experiment with the methods described by Professor Lovibond and Dr. Caddy. In order to try to enhance the effectiveness of the method, Beatrice Rouse, my research associate, and I decided to broaden the scope of the treatment. Not only did we imitate everything that they had done, but we added group therapy, family therapy, sending patients home with breath alcohol detecting devices, and so on. In other words, we developed what I have called a "blunderbuss technique" that provided everything that should be necessary to the alcoholic in learning successfully to control his or her drinking.

The patients that we accepted into this program were, with one exception, people who appear to have met the criteria for primary alcoholics. I say this in retrospect, since some of the research studies enabling us to differentiate primary and secondary alcoholics had not yet appeared. Our patients were required to spend several hours every Wednesday night drinking in our laboratory setting, which was furnished to resemble a living room of a home. The only difference between ours and the average home was that there was a one-way mirror behind which a medical student could observe all that was going on and could hear all that was being said. The patients, of course, knew about all of this. Electrodes were attached to the faces of the patients so that the medical student could push a button in the other room and deliver a personally selected electric shock that each individual had identified as unpleasant but not unacceptable. Our patients quickly learned to identify their blood alcohol levels when we provided them with feedback from the breathtesting apparatus. In addition, the evenings were spent in detailed discussion of events leading to drinking, how the family could help, how to establish control at home, and so on. Some of our patients decided that this program called for too much effort and that it would be easier just to quit altogether. Others, still feeling that controlled drinking was preferable to abstinence, toughed it out. Eventually we had a modest group of people who completed the course as we had planned it. At the end of that time they all believed that their drinking was under control, and, in the case of those who had a spouse who had participated, there was support and encouragement within the household. Our next task was to sit back and see what happened in years to come. We had carried this evening clinic program from 1970 until 1972, and we waited until 1975 to do our follow-up study so that there would be adequate opportunity for our patients either to be controlled drinkers or to relapse. When we carried out our follow-up study, we discovered that *all* of our patients had relapsed back into their former drinking styles of alcoholic drinking. Some of the patients had been rehospitalized for their alcoholism, others had decided to become total abstainers, and not one of them was drinking in a manner that could be called social drinking or controlled drinking.

This report may seem pessimistic, but it is offered mainly to try to convince the alcoholic that the probability of his or her becoming a controlled drinker is miniscule. Recently I had a conversation with Dr. Caddy, who has been interested in continuing studies of this approach. Indeed, he has done an independent evaluation of the work of another research team (Mark and Linda Sobell) who have also tried to induce controlled drinking in alcoholics. Dr. Caddy told me that many patients seem to become so frustrated with their failed attempts to be controlled drinkers that eventually they choose to become abstainers.

I have provided these details because the average alcoholic who is reading this chapter really has no personal need to undergo an entire series of failures before deciding that total abstinence is preferable. Twenty-five years ago there was a strong belief among people in the alcoholism field, including members of Alcoholics Anonymous, that one had to "hit bottom" before emerging from alcoholism into sobriety. For many people, this meant loss of job, family, friends, and perhaps even becoming a resident of "Skid Row." This belief has, fortunately, become much less firmly maintained. Now, we know that many people, either because of personal appraisal or outside coercion, can learn to do something about their alcoholism without descending all the way into social degradation. Similarly, alcoholics who are reading this chapter do not need the personal experience of trial, hope, and failure again and again with regard to drinking control before deciding on total abstinence.

To sum up, if you are a primary alcoholic, forget about drinking. Focus your goals on learning to live happily without alcohol, probably with the help of Alcoholics Anonymous.

If you are a secondary alcoholic or a careless drinker, see if you can develop control and be a responsible and careful drinker. If you cannot, then you should define yourself as an alcoholic and go for total abstinence. If you can maintain control, then good luck, provided it is lifelong.

Everything I have said so far has been directed at lifestyle, way of living, Alcoholics Anonymous, and sobriety. However, you should know that your physician has the potential for helping you with your drinking with one important drug. The medication is known as *disulfiram* and is sold under the trade name of Antabuse. If you are having problems with constantly losing your good resolutions not to drink, then having this medication in your body will help to support your decision. Once you have swallowed the Antabuse pill, you know that you cannot drink without having a very unpleasant physical reaction, and this knowledge helps you to maintain your decision not to drink. When my patients are starting on Antabuse, they sign a contract that tells them what they need to know about it: a copy of that contract is included in Chapter 26 for your information and perhaps even for the information of your doctor, should he or she not already know about how to use this medication.

chapter twenty-four

The Alcoholic

Spouse,

Parent,

or Child

Suppose someone in your family is showing clear signs of suffering from alcoholism. This chapter looks at some of the things you can do that might be helpful. There is a later chapter on the subject of someone you love who may be drinking too much but may not yet be alcoholic.

In the first place, you must realize that an attitude of loving concern rather than one of criticism and guilt provocation is more likely to be helpful. Keep focusing on the health issues of excessive drinking, and remember that your alcoholic is afraid of what life would be like without the buffer of alcohol to produce a changed state of consciousness. Try to supply facts, not threats. Information about alcohol and drinking should be available to the alcoholic: a book like this one is ideal, if they can be persuaded to read it. Although they might not read the book on request, just leaving it lying around might eventually arouse their curiosity.

Another thing to keep in mind is that the alcoholic is relatively unreachable when drinking. Thus, sometimes the mornings can be a good time for serious discussion—before the alcoholic has become badly intoxicated. If you talk with the alcoholic when he or she is intoxicated, the tendency will be for them to tune you out, and in any case their memories of the talk will be impaired.

Now, let us take some special instances. In the first place, if you are a child living at home with one or more alcoholic parents, you are in a situation that has major effects on your life style. It may be difficult for you to study at nights, and almost certainly you are less inclined to bring your friends home because of what they may see and hear. This may mean that you will have to develop a life style that involves being away from home more than would otherwise be necessary. Continue to try to have close friends, and if some of these are in the same situation, this may provide a good opportunity for comparing notes. This is one of the principles of the Alateen Group meetings, which are intended for the children of alcoholic homes. Other sources of support and understanding can include the family doctor, a school guidance counselor, a teacher, a neighbor, or a minister. It is important for you to understand that you are not the cause of the alcoholism of your parent, and, because of this, you cannot cure it. However, as already indicated, you can show your loving and optimistic concern. Try thinking about it like this: "What if my parent were a severe diabetic and failing to stick to his or her diet?" In a very real sense, the alcoholic is in a similar situation. Thus, your position should be one in which you express concern about the health issues of alcoholism and talk about sources of help such as are described in various sections of this book.

Eventually, you must leave home, and as you establish your independence it is important to keep in mind that you cannot be responsible for the health or happiness of your parents.

Next, let us consider the person with an alcoholic spouse. Again, the principles of expressing love and concern rather than criticism must apply. By all means, leave literature about alcoholism lying around, and most certainly start going yourself to meetings of Al-Anon. This organization is specifically for the spouses of alcoholics and can provide a major source of support, information, and even inspiration.

If you are trying to get your spouse to obtain outside help with the alcoholism, try to be certain that it is from someone who understands the nature of the illness. There are some psychologists and psychiatrists who are aware of how best to diagnose and treat alcoholism, but unfortunately the training of some of them left gaps in their understanding. Thus, an alcoholic spouse is likely to obtain faster and more direct help if seen by a professional who is associated with a special alcoholism clinic. Just going to a psychiatrist or a psychologist in private practice may lead to initial attempts at psychotherapy, instead of properly establishing the diagnosis.

This is also a useful time to make the point that psychoanalysis is only rarely indicated for alcoholism. Psychoanalysts are specially trained to carry out the process of analysis that helps the patient to look at the formative forces in his or her psychological development. It is a lengthy and complex process that can be very helpful in certain people suffering from psychological problems and character disorders. However, a therapy that in effect says, "Why do you do what you do?" is most certainly not indicated in cases of primary alcoholism any more than one would ask a diabetic why he or she suffers from diabetes. In addition to being a medical doctor and a trained psychiatrist, I am also a qualified psychoanalyst, and, therefore, I can give you the above advice based upon my personal knowledge and without fear of being criticized by other analysts for talking about something with which I am unfamiliar.

No counseling or psychotherapy is indicated or is likely to be useful as long as the alcoholic is still drinking. This is not to say that counseling aimed at helping him or her to stop drinking is useless. Clearly, that is needed, along with discussion of detoxification programs, rehabilitation centers, and outpatient clinic facilities. However, attempts at psychotherapy with an individual who is in an alcoholic fog are a waste of time. If an individual suffers from apparent psychological problems (examples would be anxiety, depression, insomnia, and lack of confidence) and is drinking heavily, the heavy drinking may be the root of the problem. In other words, once the individual stops drinking, the other symptoms disappear in a matter of weeks or months. A trial abstinence under these circumstances is always indicated, since it is much simpler, cheaper, and less time consuming than psychotherapy. Also, psychotherapy in the continued presence of drinking is likely to be ineffective.

One of the worst possible combinations is when there are two alcoholic spouses living together. Sometimes each declares that the other is an alcoholic while protecting their own excessive drinking with a mask of denial. Sometimes there is an unspoken arrangement whereby the marriage partners alternate in their drinking, with each taking care of the other during benders. If you live in such a situation and genuinely want to get out of it, then your own participation in Alcoholics Anonymous may be the most useful thing you can do. Everything in this chapter applies equally to yourself and to your spouse.

Marital violence is often spawned by alcoholism and should clearly be brought to the attention of legal authorities. This is especially true when the violence descends upon children within the family. Sometimes the only logical thing to do is to get away for a day or two by moving (with children, when appropriate) to a motel or going to live with a friend or relatives. Unfortunately, sometimes the authorities find themselves thwarted by the fact that the complaining spouse may refuse to press charges once the drinking has stopped, however temporarily, and will return home for a brief period of peace before the violence breaks out again. Such people, whether male or female, must be seen as possessing a streak of masochism for which some counseling or psychiatric or psychological care may be indicated.

Sometimes I see a wife who is truly locked into an alcoholic marriage by virtue of the fact that she has small children and is totally financially dependent upon her alcoholic husband. Such women sometimes argue that they cannot escape from the situation that they are in. Of course, this is not always true, and counseling with an attorney may be indicated. Also, there are social services and family service agencies available nearly everywhere. Thus, the wife who argues that she has to put up with a drinking husband who repeatedly blacks her eyes and breaks her ribs is herself suspect of at least some element of voluntary participation in the scenario. What should she do? An obvious goal, be it short-range or long-range, is to strive to achieve enough independence so that she can separate from her husband and survive with her children outside of this alcoholic marriage. Anything she can do to increase her options is to be encouraged. Sometimes this involves acquiring more education or getting a part-time or full-time job. Once she feels less locked into the alcoholic marriage she will be in a better position to improve things or to get out, should the latter be indicated.

Sometimes a separation can be truly a "therapeutic separation."* The objective is to put some pressure on the alcoholic, who, assuming that he or she values the marriage, is given time to do something about the drinking before a reconciliation is considered. If they fail or refuse to do anything about the drinking during a reasonable period of separation, such as 6 to 12 months, then the refugee spouse may reasonably start planning a permanent separation.

In general, there still are sex differences when it comes to separating out of alcoholic marriages. Men with alcoholic wives are more likely to leave than women with alcoholic husbands. Long-range statistics on what usually happens are not readily available. Professionals in the field are often amazed at how much punishment some wives will take from alcoholic husbands without escaping from the marriage. Social, sexual, and economic factors appear to make it somewhat easier for the husband to achieve separation from the alcoholic wife. One recent follow-up study showed that from 6 to 12 years after such a marriage was identified, only one-third of the marriages

*I discussed this at some length in *Marital and Sexual Counseling in Medical Practice*, 2d ed., edited by D.W. Abse, E.M. Nash, and L.M.R. Louden (Hagerstown, Maryland: Harper & Row, 1974). See chapter 13, "How to Help the Alcoholic Marriage."

were still intact, with another third ending in divorce or permanent separation and another third terminated by death of either or both partners.

Another important issue to be considered is that of remarriage and reentering into a similar arrangement, that is, another alcoholic marriage. Of course, this does not always happen, but it has happened often enough to impress many professionals that something other than chance is operating. Those who take a psychodynamic view feel that women who have more than one alcoholic husband are somehow repeatedly putting themselves in a position to be hurt and punished. The phenomenon is known as *assortative mating* and may merely represent that one tends to be comfortable with what is familiar. Various studies of women in alcoholic marriages have shown that they have a greater than average tendency to have come from an alcoholic family with an alcoholic father and/or alcoholic brothers. If this is your background and you have been married to an alcoholic, be warned of the probability that you are attracted to men with the propensity to have problems with alcohol.

Finally, no one, male or female, should ever marry with the intention of "reforming" another individual. If someone is already showing signs of alcoholism before marriage, then this merely predicts that the alcoholism will continue and even get worse after marriage.

Now, let us suppose that you are the concerned parent of a grown child who is living away from home and is showing signs of alcoholism. Many of the things already said in this chapter still apply. Be sure that he or she has the facts and knows about the specialized forms of help that are available. If there is a spouse, be certain that that person knows about Al-Anon and reads this chapter. Frustrating as it is for you to discover, there is not much that you can do to help your child with this problem, particularly if they are geographically separated from you. Pleading and criticism will fall on deaf ears and therefore should be replaced with loving concern, a focus on health, and making sure that the individual knows where to turn for help when the time comes. As the concerned parent of an alcoholic child, you, too, should start attending meetings of Al-Anon.

Suppose that you are yourself an adult and are concerned by the alcoholism of your parent or parents who are living elsewhere and are perhaps retired. Possibly this is the continuing alcoholism to which you were exposed as a child. However, as explained in an earlier chapter, bored and frustrated older people sometimes become alcoholics, and the problem is especially great if they live alone. If they live apart from you, you have less likelihood of successfully demanding change than if they live in your home. For example, if a drinking father or mother lives in your home and perhaps disturbs the household, it is perfectly reasonable for you to insist on their going to be detoxified and even going on to a rehabilitation center, since you can reasonably state what behavior is unacceptable in your home. On the other hand, if your parent lives apart from you, there may be little that you can do directly other than follow the principles outlined in this chapter and in other sections of this book.

Consider, in the case of an alcoholic grown child or an alcoholic parent, whether there are sources of coercion that can be brought to bear. The ideal source of pressure is the concerned employer who says that continued employment is dependent upon improved performance and who insists that the alcoholic must get professional help. Other possible sources of coercion include neighbors, friends, the physician, and the minister. Things may seem almost hopeless if your parent feels useless, unwanted, and is not bothered by the idea that heavy drinking will hasten death. Anything that anyone can do to help him or her to find a purpose in life is indicated. Here again, contact from a member of Alcoholics Anonymous can prove inspiring. I have seen many older alcoholics become devoted members of Alcoholics Anonymous; the meetings, the steps, and the traditions begin to provide a purpose for useful, optimistic, and happy living.

chapter twenty-five

The Drinking

Employee

If you are the owner or manager of a small business and become aware that an employee is drinking on the job, it may be very tempting to fire him or her on the spot. However, surprising as it may seem, my professional experience has taught me that frequently the employer will choose to ignore or tolerate the problem. This is particularly true with the blue-collar employee who is paid on an hourly basis. In such a circumstance, one will often hear statements such as, "Oh, sure, Joe misses a lot of work when he's on the booze, but he's really a good hard worker when he is on the job."

Both dismissal and toleration of the drinking are inappropriate. To dismiss someone who is sick seems unfair, and it may be robbing the business of a trained and useful employee who can be returned to a state of efficiency. To tolerate the drinking employee is to rob the business of a potentially efficient person while allowing that person to damage his health further and possibly to reach an irreversible stage.

The majority of adults value their employment very highly because this represents the major time investment in their life, other than the family, and it is a primary form of identification. Thus, when you first meet him, a man is much more likely to identify himself as an insurance agent, a school teacher, or a supermarket manager than to tell you that he is a husband and the father of a son and daughter. This means, of course, that the employer or supervisor has significant leverage when it comes to demanding that a worker must obtain help with health problems.

If the worker is on the job regularly, performs efficiently, and shows no deterioration compared with five or ten years earlier, then his or her behavior off the job need be no concern of the employer. However, in the case of heavy excessive drinking and alcoholism, the private life behavior inevitably begins to infringe upon work performance. This employee may come to work late, miss Monday mornings altogether, and perhaps have a faithful spouse call in various excuses on his or her behalf. Such a spouse, incidentally, is really doing the alcoholic no favor in the long run.

Other signs of the alcoholic employee include shaky hands, particularly in the morning, memory problems, and overall falling off in performance of duties. Even in situations in which it might appear to be almost impossible for the employee to drink surreptitiously, this can occur quite successfully. The alcoholic employee may carry liquor with him or her and have a quick belt during trips to the restroom. Thus, smelling alcohol on the breath is a possible sign of a drinking problem. Such people tend to be immoderate in other aspects of life, such as smoking heavily and drinking a lot of coffee. If they are in a position to go out for lunch, this may provide an opportunity for several drinks, meaning that the lunch time is likely to be prolonged and the employee is likely to be careless, dull, and perhaps soporific in the afternoon, possibly even displaying slurring of speech.

People with much experience in these work situations have learned that it is best for the employer or supervisor or foreman not to confront the employee with accusations of being "an alcoholic." On the other hand, particularly if there is potentially dangerous equipment involved, any evidence that the individual is drinking on the job can and should be presented. Very often the employee believes that no one is aware of the drinking. The major focus of such a confrontation between employer and employee should be on work safety, efficient performance, and concern about health. If deterioration in performance can be documented, so much the better. This will make it possible to measure the return to former levels of efficiency.

In some situations it may be entirely appropriate to insist on giving the employee a brief leave of absence in order to initiate a plan involving diagnosis and treatment. This is particularly true when an employee has been drinking on the job and working around hazardous machinery. In some instances, a warning letter or a document spelling out what is expected of the employee is necessary.

The main thing that should concern the employer is to have the employee return to acceptable levels of performance. How this is accomplished should be left to the employee, but he or she should certainly be offered guidance and advice. A book such as this one not only assists individuals in overcoming their denial of alcohol problems, but provides guidance about sources of help. If your business has a medical consultant, it may be appropriate to ask the employee to see the physician. Some large industrial concerns have medical departments that employ full-time physicians and nurses, and many of these have developed extremely successful plans for diagnosing and helping employees with alcoholism. With appropriate coercive measures coming from the employing organization, successful rehabilitation and return to efficient work performance have been accomplished in over 80 percent of cases that are on record. This is in contrast to the abysmally low rates of successful rehabilitation for homeless men who are out of work and thus unable to benefit from the outside pressure provided by a concerned employer.

If you are running a small business that has no medical consultation available, you can, of course, ask a suspected alcoholic employee to see his or her physician. However, in many cases it will be possible for you to obtain consultative advice from people with special experience with alcoholism in industry. One way to obtain this help is to contact the alcoholism program that exists in your local community, possibly as a component of a local community Mental Health Center. If you do not know how to reach this source, consider contacting the local department of Public Health or department of Social Services. At a state level, there is undoubtedly a state Alcoholism Authority, probably within a Department of Human Services, that can be tracked down with a few phone calls to your state government offices. All states are supposed to have special consultants who are experts on industrial alcoholism. At a national level, you can obtain advice and help in making more local contacts through the National Institute on Alcohol Abuse and Alcoholism. Chapter 34 of this book provides useful suggestions and addresses.

As is explained elsewhere in this book, some alcoholics and excessive drinkers can be successfully detoxified without admission to a hospital. However, there will be some who require a leave of absence, possibly to spend some time in a professional rehabilitation program that involves being a resident, initially on a 24-hour per day basis. Many employees are covered by health insurance programs of various kinds, and many of these provide some coverage for the treatment of alcoholism. Also, when our politicians finally stop arguing among themselves and provide our long-awaited National Health Insurance program, this will undoubtedly provide assistance in the treatment of alcoholism.

The drinking executive

Most of what I have said so far would apply to the employee who is working in a typing pool or on an assembly line, in a generally observable place with some potential for evaluation of work output, including accuracy. Unfortunately, this does not apply to the business tycoon or executive who may spend long periods of time shut in his or her office alone, protected by secretaries from interruption. Such guardian angels may quite often be aware that the executive is drinking heavily or perhaps dosing himself (and even overdosing himself) with tranquilizers and sedative drugs. Obviously, employees who protect such an executive from detection are doing the executive and the business more harm than good. On the other hand, sometimes they do not know where to turn. Only the specific circumstances of a specific case can determine this. Sometimes a confidential private secretary can talk with the boss about his apparent health problems. On occasion, it may be appropriate for such a secretary to call and speak with the wife or husband of the executive. Sometimes there is someone higher up in the organization who should be apprised of what is going on. Perhaps there is a medical department that calls for annual examinations, and an appropriate tip to the physician could be passed along in confidence.

Where the alcoholic is the owner of the business, maybe the only appropriate people to offer guidance and intervention will be his friends, family, and business acquaintances. Such people should read the chapter on getting help for alcohol problems. I have seen businessmen ruin and lose their own businesses because of their alcoholism, but I have also seen examples in which kindly and concerned pressure from outside did not come too late.

The drinking professional

In Chapter 21 I alluded to various professions in terms of drinking. The physician, dentist, attorney, or other professional who is in solo private practice is often particularly difficult to reach when alcohol problems develop. In times that are now becoming history, such people often had to go severely downhill to the point that they came to the attention of authorities before anything was done. Thus, the drinking physician would have to commit some flagrant professional errors in order to be drawn to the attention of the Medical Licensing Board, which would then either threaten to remove the license or actually do so. Fortunately, we are now seeing the development of programs among fellow professionals who assist in the identification and rehabilitation of alcoholics.

A typical plan, in the case of physicians, involves the State Medical Society. Allegations that a physician is using drugs or alcohol to excess can be confidentially passed along to some specific individual at the Society's headquarters. Such allegations may come from a fellow physician, a pharmacist, a patient, or even a family member. The next step is for a medical society committee to investigate the possible truth of these allegations, obviously doing their best to eliminate any complaints that are merely malicious. Usually, however, some discreet questioning of fellow professionals in the same local area will quickly uncover evidence that Dr. So and So has been observed acting inappropriately or in states of apparent intoxication.

The next step is for the doctor to receive a letter telling him that two members of the medical society committee wish to come and talk to him. Often one of these will be a specialist in working with drug and alcohol problems and the other will be, himself or herself, a physician who is recovering from such problems with perhaps many years of sobriety already accomplished. Such a visiting team then engages in confrontation with the physician, presenting him or her with evidence that there is a problem, but not violating the confidentiality of the sources of complaints. A discussion of appropriate steps for a rehabilitation program ensues, and in many cases the medical society arranges for a local colleague to act as a monitor to ascertain that the impaired physician is following through with a treatment plan and is continuing to show evidence of recovery.

Of course, sometimes such a confrontation leads to angry denial, or promises to seek help are not carried out. Under such circumstances, the voluntary type of program briefly described above is usually abandoned, and the more coercive possibilities involving confrontation with the State Medical Licensing Authorities are set in motion.

Not all areas already have such a mechanism established,

but state medical societies are being encouraged to develop them, and the American Medical Association is showing constructive leadership in the area. I have heard of similar arrangements being developed by dental societies, bar associations, and other groups of professionals who are concerned about developing a mechanism for assisting the solo practitioner to get onto the road of recovery from alcoholism.

chapter twenty-six

Getting

Help

for Drinking

Problems

If you do not know about locally available help, one of the first places to look may be your telephone directory. I live in a relatively small community, and yet in the white pages I can find four different numbers for Alcoholics Anonymous, as well as a listing for a private organization that offers therapy, education, and consultation on alcoholism. The AA listing includes one number for information only and another to be called on Sundays and holidays. Then, in the Yellow Pages under the heading "Alcoholism Information and Treatment Centers" I can find a listing for a private treatment program, a publicly funded crisis intervention and counseling service, Alcoholics Anonymous, an alcohol detoxification program, a "halfway house" for alcoholics run by the local Mental Health

Center, and two listings for the Mental Health Center itself, including one for 24-hour emergencies.

For many people who are drinking to excess or "alcoholically," the primary problem is recognizing the need for help and learning to accept outside help. Many of the sections of this book are addressed to that problem, and I have suggested how friends, family, and others can sometimes help the alcoholic to perceive the need. There will be occasions when concerned individuals must accept that the alcoholic is not yet ready to seek help. However, circumstances change rapidly, and this might not be true tomorrow, or next week, or next month.

For the individual who is currently drinking heavily and who experiences discomfort on stopping drinking or who is unable to go on drinking because of unwanted effects such as the vomiting and nausea of gastritis, detoxification is indicated. This might be accomplished at home with the help of a concerned relative and possibly with the assistance of some medication from the local family doctor. Be warned, however, that such medication should be for a short period of time. It must not be continued beyond a few days, otherwise it can begin merely to substitute for alcohol by creating a dependence on the medication.

Alcoholism programs, such as are available in many communities, often provide detoxification services, including 24-hour hospital care over several days to enable the individual to be thoroughly "dried out." The same can be accomplished in a general hospital under the care of a physician. Also, there are some private hospitals that specialize in such drying out services. Many programs depend upon the use of medication to substitute for the alcohol, with gradual withdrawal of the drugs. However, in recent times some so-called "nonmedical detox centers" have appeared. Such programs are based on the finding that not all alcoholics require medication in order to stop drinking. Some can stop successfully when admitted to a program that takes them away from the usual drinking locations and supplies large amounts of tender, loving care along with doses of support and encouragement. Often patients who have already been dried out but have not yet left the center can provide the kind of encouragement and reassurance that is necessary to the patient who has recently stopped drinking. Although these programs are usually called "nonmedical," they normally have someone in charge who is capable of recognizing when convulsions are occurring or are threatening, as well as when delirium tremens is impending or present. Under such circumstances, the usual arrangement is to transfer the patient to a medical setting.

The main problem with detoxification programs, necessary though they are, is that a certain number of patients use them just to get well enough again to return to drinking. This is the phenomenon that can be described as "the revolving door" and gives rise to a certain amount of despair and pessimism among the staff. However, the same is true in any aspect of an alcoholism treatment program, and staff members need to take a realistic view of alcoholism as a chronic relapsing disease, and not one that always responds favorably to initial therapy. I often point out to discouraged staff members that even though a patient may be admitted for perhaps the fifteenth time in only as many months, each individual admission is one less toward the final detoxification that will lead to his or her entering into a longer-range rehabilitation plan.

During the later stages of detoxification, every effort should be made to get the patient started in a long-range treatment plan. Obviously, educational information about health hazards must be supplied, as well as contacts with people from the rehabilitation programs, and in some cases it may be appropriate to transfer a patient directly from detox to a residential treatment program where he or she can stay dry and in initial in-patient therapy for up to several weeks. It has been my experience that most alcoholics have relatively little problem with not drinking under the circumstances of being in a rehabilitation hospital. They are away from the usual stresses and strains of everyday living and are not exposed to the same cues that trigger drinking in their everyday life. Of course, one of the dangers on discharge to the home will be reexposure to these cues and reexperiencing a craving to drink, thus relapsing into a new bout of alcoholism. There are various ways of diminishing the probability of such relapses. Many of the residential treatment programs use the time that the patient is in the hospital setting to provide much information along with a new mental set that will assist in avoiding relapse. Some treatment programs are essentially Alcoholics Anonymous oriented, where all or many of the staff are successfully recovering alcoholics themselves. In such institutions the individual is exposed to a program that can be truly inspirational and can enable many patients to experience a change of heart relative to alcohol and their way of life. A key point behind this is the reiteration of the fact that, as alcoholics, sufferers are powerless to handle alcohol safely and therefore must learn to live in a state of total abstinence. They have to become convinced that even a few sips of beer or a glass of wine will inevitably start up a craving for more liquor and thus provoke an eventual relapse. When the patient leaves the treatment center, it is with a good introduction to Alcoholics Anonymous and with the intention of becoming very much involved in regular attendance at AA meetings. As I have said elsewhere in this book, for many patients who thoroughly accept the AA program and expose themselves to it adequately, no other treatment may be necessary. This is particularly true of those who meet the criteria for primary alcoholism. If the alcoholism is superimposed on psychiatric problems such as depression or anxiety attacks, the AA program may suffice to take care of these also. However, such patients may require additional help, such as antidepressant medication for depressive illnesses or psychotherapeutic help for attacks of anxiety.

Other types of treatment facilities exist. Some of these do involve some exposure to Alcoholics Anonymous, for example, by holding an AA meeting on the premises one evening a week. However, the degree of commitment to the AA program can vary markedly. Some treatment programs may employ some recovered alcoholics as professionals or paraprofessionals while others have no alcoholics on the staff. There are real advantages to having some recovered alcoholics around in any treatment program, since these people can often empathize more directly with the alcoholic and sometimes they are better able to break through the process of denial, for example by saying such things as, "Ten years ago I was just like you, trying to kid myself and others that I was just a heavy drinker and that I could stop if I wanted to."

Many state-operated and private residential treatment programs tend to be less oriented towards Alcoholics Anonymous, although they do not necessarily reject the AA approach. Treatment in such centers will often involve watching films and television tapes on the effect of alcohol on the body, lectures about alcohol and alcoholism, group therapy meetings, and individual counseling or psychotherapy sessions. As I have indicated in various parts of this book, psychotherapy is only *sometimes* indicated for alcoholism and is *never* a treatment in itself because it cannot substitute for stopping drinking.

Other in-patient treatment programs mainly invoke behavior therapy, principally with a program of aversive conditioning. The principle behind this is Pavlovian conditioning. The individual learns to associate unpleasant physical consequences with the smell and taste of alcoholic beverages. Some hospitals use such an approach as one aspect of a spectrum of therapeutic measures, while others rely almost totally on aversive conditioning. What happens is that the patient is given alcoholic beverages to swallow while also receiving injections that make him or her vomit and feel nauseated and quite sick shortly thereafter. Sometimes the emetic medication is replaced with uncomfortable, but not dangerous, electric shocks, and some places have even experimented with injections that make the individual temporarily lose the capacity to breathe, thus making him feel that he is smothering. A combination of emetic aversive conditioning and electric shock is used in some hospitals. Drastic though these measures may seem, they are highly acceptable to some patients, providing a relatively quick access to a state in which they no longer feel a craving for alcoholic beverages and may even feel a fear of them.

Good scientifically controlled studies of the aversive therapy approach are scarce, and it has not been demonstrated that such a treatment program can provide a long-lasting aversion toward alcoholic beverages in all people. Nevertheless, the private treatment hospitals that mostly employ this technique tend to see professional and executive patients who are well motivated to overcome their alcohol problem and who there-

fore often do very well when followed up months and years later.

The issue of motivation is a crucial one in any plan of treatment for an alcoholic. I have seen patients who were coerced into entering hospitals with aversive conditioning programs and who were assured by the therapists that they were thoroughly conditioned to feel nauseated at the thought of drinking. They themselves allegedly believed this when they were discharged from the hospital. Yet, within hours or days, they relapsed. One such patient told me that he did indeed vomit up most of the first whiskey that he drank; he then lost about half of the second one, but by the time he got to the third one he was able to keep it all down, having successfully overcome his supposedly built-in aversion to his favorite alcoholic beverage.

Another important form of therapy involves the patient voluntarily taking a drug that will make him violently sick if he should drink. This is not aversive therapy, but deterrent therapy. The drug is disulfiram, known in this country as Antabuse. This is a prescription medication that should only be taken by patients who know what they are swallowing and who fully understand the side effects and the dangers of drinking. This is one medical approach to alcoholism that has been relatively neglected by the medical profession, yet it can provide many patients with a secure feeling of, "I know I can't drink, and therefore I will not drink." Patients who have repeatedly relapsed after attempts to cut down their drinking can now concentrate on the business of daily living, instead of struggling, perhaps many times a day, with the question of whether or not to take that first drink.

When I am starting a patient on Antabuse, I do so only after the patient and I have become convinced that he or she suffers from alcoholism and needs to stop drinking. Thus, it is very rare for me to start a patient on this medication at the time of the first interview. More often, we have established a good working doctor-patient relationship implying a therapeutic alliance in which we both have the same goal—namely, the reestablishment of health and control over the craving to drink. When the time comes for the patient to start the medication, I use a contract that I have advocated for physicians in general to follow. The contract reads as follows:

I, the undersigned, accept disulfiram (Antabuse) therapy as a means of deterring myself from drinking alcoholic beverages. I recognize the dangers that are connected with drinking alcohol in any form, whether in beverages, cough mixtures, vitamin tonics or any other substance containing alcohol. I also realize that some other medications such as paraldehyde, metronidazole (Flagyl), or phenytoin (Dilantin) may cause problems. Therefore, any time a doctor is prescribing for me I will tell him that I am taking Antabuse so that he can avoid giving me any other drug that might cause a bad reaction.

I understand that the reaction that occurs if a person drinks after taking Antabuse is one involving much discomfort and sickness. This can include flushing of the face, sweating, throbbing in the head and neck, palpitations, breathing difficulty, nausea, vomiting, dizziness, blurring of vision, and usually a significant fall in blood pressure. While fatalities are uncommon, death could occur in someone who drinks while taking Antabuse.

For these reasons, I will notify my family that I am taking this medication so that there will be no danger of my accidentally taking any alcohol. I will carry a card stating that I am on Antabuse. It will give recommendations for treatment of the reaction to alcohol should it occur. Should I forget to take a dose, I can safely take it as soon as I remember. However, I must never increase the dose unless my doctor advises it. If I experience any unusual and persistent feelings or symptoms, I will contact my doctor so that he can determine if they may be related to the medicine.

I fully understand that attempting to drink small amounts of alcohol while taking Antabuse is a dangerous method of trying to control excessive drinking. Not only are there potentially dangerous physical effects, but the long-term effect may be to provoke a significant degree of emotional depression.

I agree to inform Dr. _____ in advance should I wish to stop taking the medication, so that this can be fully discussed and family members informed.

I understand that the possibility of a reaction may last for many days (up to 14) after stopping Antabuse, should I take an alcoholic beverage thereafter. Should I want to commence

chapter twenty-seven

Summing

It All Up

If you have specific questions that are not answered in this book, you probably have an Alcoholism Information Center in or near your community. If not, you can seek help from your State Alcohol Authority or organizations such as the National Council on Alcoholism or the federally provided National Institute on Alcohol Abuse and Alcoholism.

If you are a college student, you may wonder why there is not a chapter specifically addressed to you. However, the entire book is addressed to you, and the chapter on teenagers also applies to young adults. My other reason for not writing a special chapter on college students is that a scholarly one already exists: see Chapter 11 in the book *Drinking,* written by me and Beatrice Rouse in 1978. That book also provides special sections on social policy and legislative matters.

Much remains to be discovered about the effects of alcohol upon the organs of the body as well as about the influence of social, psychological, and biological factors that predispose some people to drink too much while protecting others from drinking at all or from excessive drinking. Research in these areas is a special concern of the university Center for Alcohol Studies that I direct. This book has drawn on current knowledge and this will be updated as research progress is made and some of the statements made herein may eventually have to be modified.

In the United States today, well over 100,000,000 of us drink, 10,000,000 suffer from drinking problems, including alcoholism, and about 40,000,000 are also victims in that they live in homes with problem drinkers. All this means that few children or adults in the United States today are not affected in one way or another by the harmful aspects of alcohol. Yet, as I have demonstrated, alcohol can provide beneficial effects. One thing you can do that would be helpful is to emphasize, whenever you get the chance, to your legislators and congressmen the importance of adequate funding for research studies of alcohol and alcohol abuse.

section three

SPECIAL

ASPECTS OF

DRINKING

chapter twenty-eight

The Hangover

The hangover is a result of drinking too much. It represents a cry of pain from the body of the person with the hangover. For those who have never experienced a hangover, the description is likely to fall far short of the reality. For those who have experienced a hangover, the following description may seem totally inadequate.

There is, of course, a personal aspect to any hangover, but in general it represents a group of bad feelings that make an individual very uncomfortable. He or she awakens from an alcoholic sleep and wishes to be back asleep again! There is likely to be a pounding headache. There may be anything from a slight queasy feeling to a state of severe nausea, with retching and vomiting. If the sufferer is not already experiencing shakiness and a general sense of irritability, this is likely to occur before long. An increased sensitivity to light and sound is also probable. Thus, noises that normally would be ignored seem to penetrate the skull, and a level of light that would normally be quite acceptable seems unbearably bright. Underlying all of these specific symptoms may be the overall feeling of the individual that, "If this is living, I would be better off dead."

Medical science has not yet pinpointed the cause or causes of hangovers. It is known that many changes in body and brain chemistry occur when alcoholic beverages are imbibed. However, which changes produce the hangover is not clear. In spite of this, there are certain things about hangovers that should be known to those who drink and particularly to those who have experienced the hangover on one or more occasions.

Those who drink a lot and have experienced a hangover in consequence are lucky in that they now know that they have been drinking too much and that future drinking should be in lesser amounts. I have met alcoholic patients who claim that they have never experienced a hangover, and I believe that we must regard them as relatively unlucky in that their particular body makeup did not permit them to get the message that they were drinking to excess.

Sometimes people wonder why anyone would ever drink again after experiencing a hangover. Indeed, one might wonder why the hangover does not produce a form of aversive conditioning such as I described in a preceding chapter. Unfortunately, it appears that the hangover is too much removed in time from the drinking episode for it to lead to some kind of Pavlovian conditioning. Even though the drinker, as a thinking human being, can make the association between the drinking and the subsequent bad feelings, in most cases it does not make him or her feel aversive toward future drinking episodes. I think we can safely assume that very few people begin drinking with the expectation of suffering a great deal the next day, but it seems clear that for some individuals, suffering is almost inevitable after drinking too much.

For some people the experience of a hangover depends not only on how much they drink, but also on what they drink.

For example, some people suffer much more if they drink one of the liquors with a strong taste, which indicates that there are more substances present than just alcohol. Bourbon whisky contains many additional substances, which are known as *congeners,* some of which apparently remain in the body for quite a long time and may be precipitants of some aspects of the hangover. People who are sensitive to drinking bourbon in terms of getting hangovers may suffer less if they drink liquors containing fewer congeners, such as vodka. On the other hand, there are individuals who experience severe hangovers following the drinking of vodka.

One question that people often ask is, "Can the hangover be prevented?" I know of no foolproof formula for this. Some people say that they never get a hangover because they take a couple of aspirin tablets before they drink. Others swear by tablets of Vitamin C. However, there are people who experience hangovers any time they drink to excess in spite of aspirin or Vitamin C.

Even though there is obviously and undoubtedly a medical factor behind the hangover, there may in addition be a significant psychological one. At least one study has shown that people who feel guilty about the drinking they are (or have been) doing report experiencing hangovers more frequently and more intensively. Thus, at present, we would have to conclude that the hangover is the final result of a mixture of psychological and biological factors. In that regard it is a psychosomatic response to the assault upon the body by excessive amounts of alcoholic beverages. If you have experienced a hangover, it means that you were drinking too much and in future drinking you should aim for significantly less total consumption.

I know of no guaranteed cure or treatment for the hangover. The person suffering from one will feel better in a matter of hours. Sometimes two or three aspirin tablets will help an individual to feel better more quickly, especially if these are taken with lots of water or milk, and provided the individual's stomach is able to accept the medication. Some people have their own favorite recipe for combating the hangover, but as I have indicated already, an ounce of prevention (in the form of drinking less the next time) is far preferable to a pound of cure in the form of hangover recipes.

The most important thing to remember is that the traditional "hair of the dog" treatment is highly undesirable. Having morning drinks to overcome the effects of drinking the night before merely postpones the alcohol withdrawal, while at the same time putting an unnecessary additional load on the liver and other body organs. If you strain a muscle and it hurts every time you move it, you automatically rest it. Think of the hangover as a similar pain expressing the hurt that came from alcohol abuse. Rest is very definitely indicated, and this means no more alcohol.

chapter twenty-nine

Driving and

Drinking

The standard catch phrase, "If you drink, don't drive, if you drive, don't drink" is simply not accurate. Large numbers of our population know this, since they do indeed drive after drinking and drink before driving. A more accurate statement would be, "If you drink *carelessly,* don't drive."

High levels of alcohol in the body are associated with significantly increased risks of an accident during driving. For example, a person with a blood alcohol level of 0.1 percent (100 mg per 100 ml of blood) is about five times more likely to be involved in an accident than when driving while sober. Such a blood level, for a person weighing 160 pounds, implies four drinks consumed within one hour; for a person weighing 120 pounds, it implies about three drinks in the same length of time. The vast majority of people who are normal social drinkers feel pretty intoxicated at this level and realize that this is a state in which they would be impaired in performing any task calling for skill. In various experimental drinking situations, I have invariably found that people with levels that are near to the 0.1 level, but below this, express amazement when I tell them that they could still legally drive an automobile in the United States.

The interesting and important thing is that the probability of having an accident does not begin to increase significantly until the blood alcohol levels are above about 0.04 percent. For a woman who weighs from 100 to 120 pounds, this would be equivalent to one can of beer or three ounces of sherry or one and one half ounces of 86 proof liquor consumed within one hour. For a man weighing about 180 pounds, it would be equivalent to twice as much alcohol consumption in the same length of time. Most social drinkers can feel the effect of this much alcohol within the body, since it makes them feel slightly "high," with some accompanying sense of relaxation and possibly some other minor symptoms, such as feeling hot or being a little bit talkative. Yet, when a person at such a level carries out a complicated task such as driving an automobile, they do so no more dangerously than when they are totally sober. Indeed, knowing that they have had a drink, they may drive a little bit more cautiously, to the point of slightly reducing the chance of an accident.

The truth is, then, that heavily drinking drivers do represent a hazard to themselves as well as to other drivers, bicyclists, and pedestrians. On the other hand, the light social drinker under the conditions described above offers no increased risk. Unfortunately, these same light social drinkers tend to be the members of juries when heavy drinkers and alcoholics are accused of driving under the influence. Knowing that they themselves have driven safely with "a slight buzz on," they are often reluctant to convict a drinking driver, particularly when the defense counsel tries to instill doubts about the accuracy of breath testing and to make statements implying that the accused is no more than a moderate drinker. I find that the average defense attorney is incredibly naive about such matters, being unaware of the relationship between amount drunk, body weight, sex, passage of time, and blood alcohol levels achieved. Thus, when the defense counsel makes statements such as, "Ladies and gentlemen of the jury, my client readily admits that he drank two beers one hour before he was apprehended," he may really believe that he is representing the facts as they occurred. From private conversations that I have had with such attorneys outside of the courtroom, I am convinced that statements of this nature are not always concocted by the attorney, but usually represent his honest attempt to quote his client. In other words, the client is the liar. I know of instances in which juries have had sufficient doubts placed in their minds to find drivers innocent of driving under the influence even though their blood alcohol levels were demonstrated to be above 0.2 percent (twice the legal limit for driving under the influence in the United States). The fact is that if we were able to get the jury members to drink enough to get to this level, some of them would be very sick, others would have passed out, and the remainder would be staggering around and holding on to fixed objects. Only experienced heavy drinkers and chronic alcoholics can successfully negotiate their bodies in an upright posture with such blood alcohol levels. Even if they are capable of getting into a car, starting the motor, and driving down the road without swerving, their capacity for mature judgement is significantly affected by such levels of alcohol, and this seems to be a major component in leading to the mistakes that give rise to accidents.

The national statistics are undeniable. Each year about 50,000 people are slaughtered on our highways, with at least half of these deaths being due to alcohol-related accidents. When we look at single vehicle accidents, such as when a driver runs off the road and hits a tree, alcohol is a factor in about 75 percent of the deaths. Alcohol can also be a significant factor in at least 60 to 70 percent of pedestrian deaths.

In the United States we tend to regard the right to drive a motor vehicle as a right that belongs to every citizen. Unfortunately, some citizens cannot utilize this right in a responsible manner. Equally unfortunate are our attitudes of complacency and ignorance that permit heavy or careless drinking and driving to go hand in hand.

Sometimes people ask me why we do not lower the legal

drinking level for those operating an automobile to the levels used in countries such as Scandinavia. The answer is that this would be fine, provided we were willing to use these levels in a realistic manner. The fact is that we do not yet use the 0.1 percent level. The law enforcement authorities at present are required to have evidence suggesting that an individual is impaired before they can test him or her. This means that a person's driving has to be obviously impaired before any action is taken. Thus, in many states, before people are taken into court for driving under the influence, they have to be significantly more impaired than they would be at the 0.1 percent level. In some instances, the average blood levels at which convictions are obtained are as high as 0.18 percent, and, as I have indicated, people have been turned loose to drink excessively and drive again with levels far higher than that.

Various countermeasures have been tried at various times and places and with varying degrees of success. However desirable though it may be to raise the public consciousness about the dangers of excessive drinking and driving, most campaigns so far have had only temporary effects that were measurable. A significant change in public attitude is called for, and this requires more public awareness of some of the facts that I am outlining here.

It appears to be possible to create an attitude that is less conducive to heavy drinking and driving. In Sweden and some other Scandinavian countries, the driving population is sufficiently aware and concerned (as well as being afraid of the inevitable consequences, such as loss of license) that one member of a group will specifically not drink in order to be able to drive the others home from a party.

A responsible host or hostess should not permit intoxicated people to drive home from their party. For that matter, the supply of alcoholic beverages should be tapered off as the evening progresses, so that people can have a chance to sober up before they drive home. Supplying coffee in the later stages of the party is all right if it encourages people to stay on and thus burn up some of the alcohol in their system. But remember that giving coffee to a drunk person in no way sobers him up directly. It has been aptly said that giving coffee to a drunk simply makes for "a wide awake drunk."

Various programs aimed at educating people about the effect of alcohol on driving may have some beneficial effects as may also laws that permit limited licensing for driving purposes so that after a conviction for drunken driving a worker can drive to and from work, for example, but not drive elsewhere in the evenings.

It is my belief that for the moment we must depend on increased public consciousness of the careless drinking and driving problem, support of existing laws, and better education of judges, attorneys, and juries. However, I believe that in the long run a technical solution must be found for the problem. I think that eventually it will become possible to develop automobiles that simply cannot be driven by a person who is in a state of impaired competence to drive. Possibly such an engineering solution will involve a task that calls for vigilance and an unimpaired state of consciousness before the motor can be started. Another possible engineering solution would be a device that prevents the car from being driven if significant amounts of alcohol are detected in the driver or if the driver fails to show the normal frequency of steering wheel correction movements or eye-scanning activity. I believe that the technical capacity to solve this problem will be developed, and that then, and only then, can we expect significant drops in highway accidents and fatalities due to careless drinking.

chapter thirty

Sex and

Drinking

For many people, small amounts of alcohol appear to be an aphrodisiac, that is, a substance that increases sexual desire or is felt by them to contribute positively to a sexual experience. Although good scientific studies to prove this point are not available, this is the general opinion expressed by many men and women.

Another source of information comes from psychotherapists who work with large numbers of patients. A majority of them express the belief that small amounts of alcoholic beverages (one or two drinks) do increase sexual pleasure or performance.

This appears to be quite in contrast with the centuries-old view expressed by Shakespeare through his character, the porter, in "Macbeth." The porter says that drink is a great provoker of three things: nose-painting, sleep, and urine. He goes on to discuss the effect of drink on sex with the following monologue: "Lechery, sir, it provokes and unprovokes: it provokes the desire, but it takes away the performance. Therefore much drink may be said to be an equivocator with lechery: it makes him, and it mars him; it sets him on, and takes him off; it persuades him and disheartens him; makes him stand to, and not stand to; in conclusion, equivocates him in a sleep, and, giving the lie, leaves him."

The explanation for these seemingly opposing views is, of course, based on the fact that alcohol, like other drugs, has different effects at different dose levels. Just as a small amount of alcohol (one or two drinks) will make many people feel relaxed, friendly, and euphoric, we also know that large amounts can provoke loud, abrasive, and aggressive behavior as well as severe deterioration in the performance of many tasks. When it comes to sex, small amounts of alcohol (one or two drinks) may enhance the experience for many people by virtue of making them feel euphoric, relaxed, and friendly, whereas large amounts may provoke uninhibited expression of sexual desire (the lechery described by Shakespeare) accompanied by a failure to be able to perform. The latter is more likely to be a problem in the case of the male, since impotence in his case means either the inability to achieve an erection or the inability to maintain one. However, impotence is not invariable, and many rapes are perpetrated by intoxicated men. Incestuous relationships are apparently often initiated while the instigator is less inhibited than usual, due to alcohol.

Alcohol is associated with the loss of inhibitions and social control and the lessening of guilt feelings. Thus, individuals who are somewhat uptight or guilty about sexual activity may feel some benefit from the moderate use of alcohol in a sexual setting. Diminished self control on the part of a woman whom he is trying to seduce is an obvious means to an end on the part of the male. Thus, plying a woman with drink as a sexual preliminary must have been used by men on millions of occasions. There may be less of a need for such a tactic today, in this age of more honest attitudes about sex, than there was in former times, when sex, guilt, and inhibition went hand in hand.

I have known males who found moderate amounts of alcohol beneficial in coping with sexual performance problems. A man with a tendency to have premature ejaculation, for example, might find this tendency much diminished after one to three drinks. The effect of the alcohol might be to reduce tension and guilt feelings or just generally to reduce overall sensitivity to stimulation so as to permit a lengthier genital contact. Perhaps both factors are involved.

There are some inevitable problems if an individual depends upon alcohol for successful sexual performance. In the first place, the constant association between sex and alcohol may eventually lead to a state in which sexual performance is virtually impossible in the absence of alcohol. Another problem is that of achieving the correct dose level. If a man discovers, for instance, that two drinks enhances sex for him, he may begin to think that four drinks will double his pleasure and six will triple it! Clearly, this is not so, and impotence can be a result. Finally, there is the fact, as I have carefully explained throughout this book, that there is no such thing as totally risk-free drinking, and there are individuals who cannot afford to drink at all.

Impotence associated with heavy alcohol use may occur because of the overall reduced sensitivity produced by the alcohol. Before anesthetic agents were discovered, a lot of surgery was conducted after getting the patient very intoxicated. Alcohol in heavy amounts can provide a degree of anesthesia. The common euphemism for intoxication, "He's feeling no pain," recognizes this fact.

Another source of impotence may be the considerable effect that alcohol has upon body hormones. The sex hormones involve complicated interactions between a specialized part of the brain and the pituitary and sex glands. Current research shows that acute doses of alcohol (single large amounts given to an experimental rat, for example) are associated with major changes in hormone levels. Of particular interest is the significant lowering of the male hormone, testosterone. Similar findings have been demonstrated in male human volunteers whose peak blood alcohol levels were at about the 0.1 percent level, above which it is illegal to drive a motor vehicle.

Long-term administration of alcohol to the experimental animal also produces many chemical responses within the body, some of which affect sex and reproduction. Human alcoholics are no exception. It has long been recognized that chronic alcoholic men suffer from atrophy (shrinkage) of the testicles and have lower levels of testosterone in the blood than normal. Some of the changes appear to represent the direct toxic effect of alcohol upon the sex glands and other endocrine (hormone secreting) glands. Other aspects of the changes in the chronic alcoholic human male may be secondary to changes in the liver. It has often been assumed that for the chronic alcoholic male, obtaining continuing supplies of alcoholic beverages is the major purpose in life and that all other interests, including interest in sex, become unimportant. This may be true for some alcoholics, but a recent study in Scotland found that alcoholics do not have a low sexual interest and drive and are quite concerned with sexual intercourse. The main difference between alcoholics and matched nonalcoholics was the fact that they described less sexual satisfaction. This appeared to be due to the lack of suitable sexual partners and to a greater degree of impotence (inability to have an erection) on the part of the alcoholics.

Women who are heavy drinkers or alcoholics also appear to suffer effects involving their sex hormones and sexual organs. Here, as in the case of the male, we simply do not yet have enough research information to be able to present the total picture. However, such women, when compared with matched controls (women of the same age and similar socio-economic background who do not use alcohol to excess) are found to have a greater history of problems involving sexuality and reproduction. In this regard, we are faced with one of these "chicken or egg" questions. In Chapter 7, I showed how both men and women with conflicts about their own sexuality may be tempted to drink more heavily and thus to feel some sense of resolution. So, in the case of the alcoholic woman, we can ask, "Does she drink heavily because of sexual dissatisfactions, or are the sexual difficulties secondary to the heavy drinking?" Although any attempt to answer this question today has to be strictly speculative, it is probable that both factors are operating in some people and possibly only one factor in others.

Although sexual desire and love making provide one of mankind's strongest sources of drive and pleasure, we must not forget that this is nature's way of continuing the species. In other words, we cannot leave the subject of sex and alcohol without considering reproduction. In the chapter on women and alcohol, I have described the fetal alcohol syndrome. There is evidence available today to indicate that heavy drinking during pregnancy is associated with less healthy babies and even permanently damaged ones. We do not even know at which time in the pregnancy alcohol is most dangerous, but it is likely that a particularly dangerous time is early in the pregnancy. If there is a totally safe amount of maternal drinking that has no effect on the outcome of a pregnancy, this is simply not known. Thus, the safest thing to say is that women should avoid alcohol when pregnant or attempting to become pregnant. On the other hand, a pregnant woman, particularly when the pregnancy is well established, should not feel guilty or worried if she sips an occasional glass of wine with a meal.

Over a hundred years ago, the idea was expressed that alcohol abuse could produce deleterious changes in the spermatozoa (germ cells) of the male. Good experiments that could prove this were lacking, but the opinion was often expressed. For example, Dr. W.A.F. Brown of the Crichton Royal Hospital in Dumfries, Scotland stated, "The drunkard not only injures and enfeebles his own nervous system, but entails mental disease upon his family. His daughters are nervous and hysterical. His sons are weak, wayward, eccentric and sink insane under the pressure of excitement of some unforeseen exigency or the ordinary calls of duty." When I was a medical student, we tended to scoff at such ideas since it was generally felt that a drunken sperm, or more correctly the millions of sperms of the drinking man, would only be less capable of fertilizing the woman's egg. Modern genetics, however, has led us to understand that various drugs and even environmental exposure to noxious agents can produce chromosomal abnormalities. Thus, I doubt if any scientist today would assert with confidence that heavy drinking in the male is without effect on the sperm he produces. Some very recent animal studies seem to have demonstrated developmental and behavioral abnormalities in the offspring of alcoholic male rats where the mothers received no alcohol during the pregnancy. If such findings are confirmed, they will raise important issues for human alcohol consumption and alcoholism. For example, Dr. Brown and his nineteenth century contemporaries may have been right. In Chapter 8, I discussed inborn factors influencing drinking and described various studies confirming the existence of an inborn factor in at least primary alcoholics. The initial adoption study carried out by Dr. Goodwin and his colleagues in Denmark involved children of alcoholics who were raised by adopting parents. In 85 percent of these children, the biological father was the alcoholic, thus only 15 percent were born to mothers who might have been drinking alcoholically during their pregnancy. There appear to me to be three possible explanations for these findings. The first is that there is some biological difference extending through many generations that increases the propensity to be alcoholic if one drinks (or at least it does not provide any protection from becoming alcoholic). Such a propensity would be present whether or not either of one's parents used alcohol. Higher rates of alcoholism among the grandchildren of alcoholic grandfathers would be compatible with this idea. The propensity may be associated with the hyperkinesia syndrome that I have described earlier in this book.

A second possibility is that the wives of alcoholic men tend to drink more heavily than the wives of nonalcoholic men during their pregnancy (perhaps trying to "keep up" with their husband's drinking). If so, this would imply that the offspring of such marriages had greater exposure to alcohol while in the womb than average, and that such exposure produces the later behavioral problems that promote alcoholic drinking patterns.

A third possibility, remote though it may have formerly seemed, is that there is some change produced in the sperm of alcoholic men that can influence the outcome of the pregnancy and thus the future of the child, should he or she later choose to drink. The sperm from the male carries one half of the biological blueprint that determines the characteristics of the offspring. If heavy drinking on the part of the father can change some parts of that blueprint, then it is possible that this is a mechanism whereby the propensity to have problems with alcohol could be passed from one generation to another. At the present time, we do not know whether any one, or even all three, of these possible mechanisms are responsible for the familial factor in alcoholism. Thus, it is clear that much more research is called for.

What does all this mean?

Meanwhile, what should we do with the facts as we have them at present? In the first place, if you and your sexual partner enjoy a drink or two as a preamble to sexual activity, go ahead—providing that the woman is not trying to become pregnant. Avoid constantly associating alcohol and sex (whether you are male or female) if you hope at some future time to father or mother a child. My reason for advising this is that you want to be able to have satisfactory sexual relationships without alcohol when the woman is trying to conceive. This means, for example, that if a man is depending upon alcohol to overcome premature ejaculation and hopes later to father a child, it may be all right if he uses alcohol less and less to establish control, but if the premature ejaculation persists, he should get some therapy for it. The therapeutic techniques developed by Masters and Johnson are now widely available throughout the country and are tremendously beneficial.

If a man or a woman is drinking heavily or is already showing signs of being an alcoholic and wishes to have a child, the desire for an offspring should be postponed until the alcohol problems are dealt with. In this book I have described how some heavy and excessive drinkers may be able to cut down their alcohol intake to acceptable levels. This is unlikely to occur in the case of the primary alcoholic, and I have demonstrated how you can decide if you meet the definition for that. If you are a primary alcoholic, or if you are unable to maintain low levels of alcohol intake, then it is *essential* to get outside help with your drinking before fathering or mothering a child. If I had written this book just a few months ago, I would have said "before mothering a child" in the preceding sentence. However, the recent animal studies that I have mentioned do raise the serious possibility that alcoholic germ cell damage in the male can be passed along to the offspring.

If you are a female who is a moderate drinker and you are trying to become pregnant, the wisest decision of all would be to stop drinking completely until the pregnancy is accomplished and you are delivered of a healthy baby. In the case of a man who is trying to father a healthy baby, there is obviously no objection to his drinking during her pregnancy once his wife has conceived. On the other hand, perhaps many prospective fathers will wish to assist their wives to abstain from alcoholic beverages by not drinking themselves.

If you are a light or moderate drinking female and discover that you are already pregnant, what should you do? Assuming that this pregnancy is acceptable and that you do not wish to seek a therapeutic abortion, your best bet is to go ahead with the pregnancy but to stop drinking. Again, please note, that stopping drinking does not mean that you cannot slowly sip an occasional glass of table wine with dinner. It does mean that you should avoid drinking enough to feel "high" or intoxicated. Remember that when you take a drink and feel intoxicated, your baby is sharing that drink, and its growing tissues may be more susceptible to the alcohol than the tissues in your body.

If you are an alcoholic woman who has been drinking heavily for months or years and who discovers that she is pregnant, what should you do? My best advice would be to talk this over promptly with your doctor and possibly to obtain special consultation with geneticists and obstetricians who are experts in this area. A good decision might be to have a therapeutic abortion followed by treatment of your alcoholism with the intention of then becoming pregnant again, knowing that this time you have reduced the risks to your baby.

What if you are a normal, healthy woman whose partner

was drinking fairly heavily at the time of the sexual intercourse that, you believe, led to the present pregnancy? Based on our present knowledge, there is little reason to believe that a single heavy drinking episode on the part of your husband would produce an unhealthy baby, and under these circumstances I think that you should let the pregnancy proceed if it is one that you desire.

What if your husband is a chronic alcoholic and succeeded in making you pregnant? Under these circumstances, as I have indicated above, there may be a possibility of some spermatic change that could influence the outcome of the pregnancy or the health of the child if it is born successfully. Here, again, some special consultation with your doctor and possibly other experts may be helpful. There is a tendency for spontaneous abortion (miscarriage) to occur if an unhealthy pregnancy is underway. However, under the circumstances that I have described, and particularly if this is not a pregnancy that you especially desire, this may justify your seeking a therapeutic abortion. Of course, if you have moral or religious scruples about therapeutic abortions and feel that you must let the pregnancy proceed, then all you can do is hope for the best. Based on our present knowledge, there is no absolute reason for you to fear that the pregnancy will not be normal and that your baby will not be absolutely healthy.

chapter thirty-one

Hospitalization

and

Drinking

I talked about special hospital treatment for alcoholism in Chapter 26; here, instead, I want to focus on the incidental relationship between drinking and hospitalization, a relationship that unfortunately has not been recognized enough by the medical profession or the general population.

Studies in this country and elsewhere regularly show that significant numbers of hospital beds are taken up with people suffering from the complications of drinking to excess. In a small rural hospital, only 3 to 5 percent of the beds may be occupied by such patients, whereas in large cities and some Veterans Administration hospitals, the percentage may be as high as 50! University hospitals that receive a lot of referrals from other hospitals regularly find that as many as 25 percent of their beds are taken up with patients whose illnesses are alcohol related. Some of these people are suffering from alcoholism while others have the organ damage that is produced by the toxic effects of alcohol intake. If the patient, on confrontation by the doctor about the role of alcohol in producing the illness, can stop drinking, then the problems will usually subside. Unfortunately, many doctors do a very poor job of this confrontation. In some cases, they may say nothing at all because they don't know how to offer help. In other instances, they may mutter something such as, "You ought to drink less," again, without offering any assistance. Some doctors merely get angry with the patient, ranting and raving about the fact that he brings his illness on himself, thus raising the problem as a moral issue rather than as a health issue. Needless to say, the patient who is made to feel guilty may well turn to alcohol for lessening of guilt feelings as soon as he discharged.

All this means that we must do a better job of educating medical students and physicians in general to recognize alcoholism, to conduct a realistic confrontation with the patient, and to offer guidance and help. At the very least, if the doctor is not prepared to continue working with the patient himself, he ought to see that a concerned and experienced physician is brought in and should provide referral to other sources of help, such as special clinics and Alcoholics Anonymous.

Another long-standing problem involving alcohol and hospitalization revolves around the "conspiracy of silence." This means that frequently the correct diagnosis of alcoholism never gets on the chart. In the old days, doctors used to try to justify this on the grounds that insurance companies would not pay for the treatment if the diagnosis of alcoholism was made. Thus, patients would frequently be admitted to the hospital for short-term detoxification with the admitting diagnosis listed as "gastritis." The correct diagnosis would have been, "alcoholic gastritis secondary to alcoholism," but although the doctor knew this, he did not write it down. The insurance situation has changed markedly in recent times and most policies now will pay for the treatment of alcoholism. Studies have shown that it is more economical in the long run to treat the alcoholism than to keep paying for a series of admissions for treatment for the complications of the alcoholism that is itself untreated.

When alcoholics and heavy excessive drinkers are admitted to the hospital on an emergency basis, their continuing supply of alcohol usually dries up. Going into a state of enforced abstinence can bring about the withdrawal syndrome, and everyone should know this. During the first 24 hours or so after admission, the patient may sweat a lot and be somewhat shaky and uncomfortable. Occasionally he may experience hallucinations, hearing or seeing things that do not really exist. Sometimes the hallucinations are quite pleasant. I have known patients to comment on the beautiful choral music that they thought was being played to them or to laugh and smile about the "cute little men" they could see running down the bedclothes, seemingly thinking that this was some kind of cartoon movie put on for their amusement. When heavy drinking has preceded this hospital admission, convulsive seizures may occur 24 to 36 hours after the drinking has stopped. Then, if the condition is not recognized and treated, we may see the development of full-blown delirium tremens. Here, the patient is extremely frightened because the things he is hearing and seeing are perceived as very threatening; patients have been known to jump out of hospital windows to get away from supposed persecutors.

Another time that the above sequence of events may be seen is following emergency surgery for some acute surgical illness. The anesthesiologist may pick up a clue that the patient is alcoholic because alcoholics generally require more anesthetic to put them to sleep, often as much as one third more than a nonalcoholic of the same size. Once the surgery is completed and the patient is going through what should be a normal recovery, the onset of the withdrawal syndrome can interfere markedly with the course of events. If the doctors still have not made the correct diagnosis, they may believe that they are dealing with a patient who has suddenly developed psychiatric symptoms and call for a psychiatric consultation. I have seen many patients under such circumstances, and the treatment of the developed condition is much more difficult and dangerous than preventing it in the first place.

This leads to the most important point in this entire chapter. If you are admitted to a hospital on an emergency basis and if you are drinking to excess, for whatever reason, tell your doctor about this. Typically the anesthesiologist sees you the night before surgery (although this will not be true if the surgery is performed under emergency conditions). However, it is vital for the physicians and surgeons who are taking care of you to know that you have been drinking a lot; they should know how much you have been drinking on a daily basis and for how long. This can enable them to take appropriate steps to get you safely anesthetized, and, during the postoperative phase, to provide medications (typically minor tranquilizers like Librium and Valium) in doses that will prevent the development of the alcohol withdrawal syndrome. Once you are past this danger point, the medications can and should be withdrawn slowly so that you proceed through the postoperative phase comfortably and without danger.

These remarks also apply if you are admitted to a hospital for investigation of illness not calling for surgery. Again, if you have been drinking heavily, your doctor should know this in order to decide if some preventive treatment is called for. What *is* heavy drinking under such circumstances will vary from person to person according to his or her size, how long they have been drinking, and how experienced they are. However, anyone who has been drinking twelve or more ounces of liquor daily for more than just a few days is going to experience some discomfort on stopping this intake. If you have been drinking from a pint to a quart daily, you are significantly at risk to develop the severe complications that are brought about by sudden stopping.

If you are being admitted to a hospital on an elective basis, that is if you are planning toward a specific date, your doctor should again know of your heavy alcohol intake so that you and he together can plan an appropriate course of action. This will mean cutting down your daily intake, for example, by using the 10 percent daily reduction intake schedule that I have described in Chapter 15. If you cannot do this on your own, your doctor may provide some assistance or will refer you to an appropriate source of help. Reducing your daily intake to a low amount, or stopping it altogether, will ensure a safer and more comfortable period in the hospital.

What about drinking in hospitals? Many doctors and some nurses will tell you that drinking does not go on in hospitals. Of course, there are some hospitals that will provide alcoholic beverages to patients on request or when prescribed by the physician. But I know that a considerable amount of surreptitious drinking goes on that is unknown to the medical staff. This is based on what patients and families have told me. Thus, alcoholics in hospitals sometimes arrange for friends or family to smuggle in continued supplies. In the case of the alcoholic patient, this can be outright dangerous. Less dangerous, in most instances, is the practice of some patients to sneak a cocktail or two before dinner. Sometimes the bedside table of the patient may be about as well stocked as the home bar! If you are not an alcoholic and simply want to continue to enjoy a drink before dinner, you really should discuss this with your doctor. There may be medical reasons against this (or in favor of it), and the alcohol intake may alter the results of some of the laboratory tests that are being performed.

There is no doubt that for many people the daily drink is perceived as contributing to the quality of life. There are some long-term hospitals and nursing homes that have learned this and make a practice of serving some sherry before dinner or a glass of wine with meals. Studies have tended to show that patients in such institutions are more appreciative and contented when compared with those that have more rigid policies. Again, it is impossible to generalize, but if the doctor feels that a small daily intake of alcoholic beverage offers no health hazard to his patient, he may feel justified in recommending it as being overall beneficial.

chapter thirty-two

Alcoholics

Anonymous

and Al-Anon

I have talked about Alcoholics Anonymous and Al-Anon throughout this book, but I feel that a special chapter is called for. If you have turned to this chapter first, then you may not yet know how favorably I feel about them. My experience, like that of most doctors, is that Alcoholics Anonymous is the single most succesful treatment plan for alcoholism when an alcoholic will accept it. Likewise, the Al-Anon organization can be a life saver and a morale booster for the spouse, family, or friend of the alcoholic. Additionally, I have referred to the Alateen movement for teenagers and in some localities we are beginning to see the development of Alatots for preteenage children with an alcoholic in the family.

When De Tocqueville studied the early United States, he

commented that here was a "nation of joiners." Group organizations have been typical of our history, but the specialized self-help group movement seems especially to be typical of the mid-twentieth century. Before Alcoholics Anonymous, programs for alcoholics tended to be help offered by others and were often aimed at the down-and-out or skid-row alcoholic. Do-gooders would provide soup kitchens, flop houses, and alcoholic farms, for example. This provided some help for that small percentage of alcoholics who are homeless and helpless, but did nothing for the other 95 percent.

From time to time various special treatment programs for alcoholism have appeared. One of the best known was the "cure" offered by the many Keeley Institutes. These were started by the enterprising Dr. Leslie E. Keeley in the last century and some operated until well into this century. Dr. Keeley's secret treatment for alcoholism involved injections by a physician who was encouraged to talk to the patients and, perhaps even more important, to listen to them. A large element of suggestion was present, and "cured" patients often testified publicly about how the treatment had benefited them. Just what percentage remained cured and what percentage was not helped at all remains unknown. Apparently the treatment offered in the Keeley Institutes evolved, so that what was originally a secret remedy (and thus a money-making plan rather than a program open to scientific verification) gradually appears to have become more like the traditional drying-out-with-counseling approach.

I will not detail the history of Alcoholics Anonymous in this chapter, but Chapter 34 suggests some further reading sources for the interested person. Suffice it to say that Alcoholics Anonymous essentially got its start when two men, both alcoholics, decided to lean upon each other and thus to help each other with their common problem. The maxim, "United we stand, singly we fall," applies to all of the self-help groups. By finding oneself no longer isolated, but a member of a group of people with a common purpose, one gains strength from the group.

From its initial tiny beginnings, the Alcoholics Anonymous movement has grown throughout this country and the world.

In the United States today, in communities of any appreciable size, AA meetings are going on seven days a week. Indeed, you would have to live in an extremely isolated area not to have an active AA group within easy traveling distance of you.

Those who have never gone to an Alcoholics Anonymous or Al-Anon meeting may need a little reassurance. In the first place, you will find yourself among a friendly sympathetic group of human beings who will accept your presence there without criticism or questioning. You will not be required to stand up and make some type of "group confession." All that will be asked of you is an open mind. For the person who is not suffering from alcoholism, attendance at an open meeting of AA can be a rewarding and an educational experience. The local doctor, minister, school teacher, or attorney who merely goes along to find out what it is all about will be welcomed. Those who decide to join Alcoholics Anonymous actively and to start participating in the closed meetings will be expected to acknowledge submission to a power greater than themselves. Most people with alcohol problems find this quite easy to do, since alcohol itself has already demonstrated its power over them. For those who have some type of religious belief in a God, this acknowledgement may be easy. Occasionally, however, I come across alcoholics who try to reject AA on the grounds that it is "a religious organization" or calls for one to believe in certain supernatural powers. In fact, this is not accurate, since all that is called for is acknowledgement of one's powerlessness over alcohol and recognition of the need to turn outside of oneself for help. The local group itself and the entire AA organization represent an outside higher power, and each individual learns to relate to the concepts of AA on an individual basis.

Some years ago I was talking to a Ph.D. who is an avowed atheist but who is an enthusiastic and successful member of Alcoholics Anonymous. I asked him how he reconciled these two things and he admitted that it took him a long time to be able to turn to AA. His alcoholism had just about hit bottom; he was feeling hopeless and defeated and decided to commit suicide. He took some drinks and sat on the top of a cliff, intending to throw himself over onto the rocks below. First, however, he sat there looking out at the ocean, studying the waves as they rolled in and the surf crashing below. A sense of peace and understanding overtook him and on the spot he acknowledged that the ocean, and indeed nature in its entirety, represented a power far greater than himself. With this new-found insight he was able to return to Alcoholics Anonymous and, this time, to achieve sobriety through its program.

The program of "twelve steps and twelve traditions" that has evolved presents the Alcoholics Anonymous member with a series of tasks that gradually help him or her to overcome the problems of living, to straighten out interpersonal relationships, and to reach for a sense of serenity while abstaining from the use of alcohol. Again, I will not attempt to detail this procedure because reading about it is not enough. Experiencing it is essential for anyone who is going to benefit from it.

Details and accurate statistics about Alcoholics Anonymous are not available, but there have been surveys that do lead to some overall information. There are probably about a million members throughout the world, with well over half a million in North America. About a third of them are women. They cover all age groups, with the majority being between ages 30 and 50, but with significant numbers below 30 and above 50. Surveys carried out from 1968 to 1974 led to the estimate that over ⅓ of those sober for less than a year in Alcoholics Anonymous will not drink again and will remain in the organization during the succeeding year. Of those who have been sober for one to five years, about ⅘ will stay sober in the fellowship. Of those who have been sober for more than five years, over 90% will never drink again and will remain in AA.

Almost all of those surveyed as members of AA reported an improvement in the quality of their lives in the areas of family, health, work, and community since their membership began. Over a third of the members are in the executive, professional, or technical categories of occupation, and about a third are blue-collar and office workers. About one-third of the members indicated that they were first encouraged to investigate the organization by counseling they received from a physician, a psychologist, or a minister. Such counselors should try to know who are members of Alcoholics Anonymous among their patients or clients. This can be very helpful in getting other patients to sample some AA meetings.

When I first identify a patient as suffering from alcoholism, I rarely feel that I have enough evidence on the first contact to tell him or her never to drink again. However, over a series of contacts we try to identify whether this is primary or secondary alcoholism and to see whether or not reliable and lasting control of the drinking can be established. Once the patient and I are convinced that this is primary alcoholism without control and that there is a need to establish total abstinence, I consistently advocate membership in Alcoholics Anonymous in addition to other treatment measures such as I discussed in Chapter 26. Rather than ask the patient just to walk into an AA meeting as a total stranger, I will ask him if I may arrange for a local AA member to phone him and arrange to take him to a meeting that night. With the patient's permission, I then telephone one of my other patients who has years of sobriety behind him; this AA member will then call the new prospective member and arrange to take him to the next meeting.

The "anonymous" aspect of AA was vital during the first two or three decades of its existence, since public and private attitudes toward alcoholism were so negative. However, in recent times we have seen famous and distinguished citizens announce that they are alcoholics; alcoholism is now better understood as an illness, and attitudes toward it are improving. Nevertheless, strictly speaking, individuals should not identify themselves as "a member of Alcoholics Anonymous." However, it is perfectly all right for an individual to identify himself or herself as "an alcoholic." Some alcoholics I know get around the problem when speaking to outside groups by identifying themselves as, "an alcoholic who found sobriety by membership in a well-known self-help group for alcoholics."

Finally, a few words about Al-Anon. This organization can offer enormous support and help to the spouse of the alcoholic, whether the latter is now sober or is still drinking. Where the drinking persists, sometimes membership in Al-Anon produces changed attitudes and behaviors that eventually bring the alcoholic into Alcoholics Anonymous. Thus, any time that someone asks "What shall I do about my alcoholic husband or wife?" the answer should be to learn as much as possible about alcoholics and alcoholism (such as by reading this book) and start attending meetings of Al-Anon. If you don't know where the local Al-Anon groups are meeting, look in the telephone book, particularly the Yellow Pages. If there is nothing listed there, ask your doctor or minister or call the local Social Services department. Unless you live in a remarkably isolated community, you will find that there is an Al-Anon group somewhere within reach.

chapter thirty-three

Loving

Someone

Who Drinks

Too Much

Previous sections of this book have described the treatment of alcoholism and have provided suggestions for those who are emotionally involved with an alcoholic and want to help. This chapter is aimed at the person who feels that a loved one is drinking too much but who may not yet need treatment for alcoholism.

If you feel that your lover, husband, wife, parent, sibling, or child is drinking too much, the first issue is to determine whether or not this is so. If your concern is about someone who lives in a different household, it may be quite impossible for you to know how much they are drinking but quite possible to learn about the effects of drinking. For example, there may be arrests for driving under the influence, a series of apparently minor car accidents, health complications, interpersonal problems, or work difficulties.

Sometimes the "drinking too much" is much more in the eye of the beholder than in the life of the drinker. On more than one occasion wives have brought husbands to me because of alleged drinking problems, and yet there really were no problems except in the mind of the wife. Thus, one wife who had had a very rigid upbringing was bothered by the fact that her husband would drink one beer, and occasionally a second one, on Sunday afternoons while watching football on television. Another wife was convinced that her husband was going on the skids because he would sometimes drink a whole six-pack of beer within a week or ten days. In instances like this, where there are no behavioral problems arising from very moderate drinking, the main hope is to get the wife to modify her attitudes, perhaps by reading this book. An alternative for the husband is for him to decide that it is easier to use soft drinks in place of beer than to have to deal with the wife's anxieties.

Now, what if it is clearly a fact that the one you love is drinking hazardous amounts with damaging effects on health, psychological makeup, interpersonal relationships, or work capacity? Here we are dealing with a problem as complex as that of the smoker who continues to smoke in spite of severe emphysema, or the obese person who continues to overeat, or the diabetic who fails to follow medical advice. Some people follow essentially self-destructive paths, and while we may understand that there are involved psychological problems behind such a course of action, we may be helpless to intervene. Where someone is clearly going in a self-destructive direction, we should try to stop it, but we should recognize our limitations.

One approach is to see that the individual is provided with the facts. For example, handing over a copy of this book in a loving and constructive way might be helpful. A suitable comment would be, "I've been reading this book and it made me wonder if you might be drinking too much for your own good. Please read it yourself and see what you think." Of course, the person whose heavy drinking is threatened by such an approach may respond with denial, but I have known instances in which such a confrontation led to realistic decisions and positive action.

If you are living in the same household with someone who is drinking too much, keep in mind that the time for any confrontation is when they are not drinking or are drinking very little. An angry scene the night before is unlikely to be helpful and may even be lost in a blackout. Some loving and concerned confrontation over breakfast coffee or while spending the weekend at the beach together is more likely to be successful.

Occasionally, you may be in a position to demand change provided you are genuinely willing to follow through with any threats you might make. For example, parents who say they will not again provide bond and legal help for their arrested son must be willing to turn a deaf ear the next time such circumstances present themselves. Likewise, the wife who announces she will move out with the children the next time her husband becomes drunk and threatening must be prepared to carry this out.

You must learn to ignore the false accusations that are thrust upon you. Loved ones who drink too much are very expert at stirring up guilt feelings in others. Thus, a daughter who drinks too much may tell her mother that it is because the mother favored her son over her daughter. A heavily drinking husband may assert that of course he drinks a lot because the children are so noisy or because his wife is so niggardly with sex. You, as someone who loves someone who drinks too much, must keep in mind that there is no evidence that *any* individual has ever made *another* individual become alcoholic. You did not "make" your loved one into an alcoholic, nor are you in the process of accomplishing this. The corollary also applies in that you cannot prevent your loved one from drinking too much or from becoming an alcoholic if he or she does not cooperate. All you can do is to see that they have the facts available and try, if you can, to get them some outside help.

I have talked about the apparent self-destructive behavior of some individuals. Sometimes the most we can do is to diminish the destructive effects upon other people. Sometimes, though, this will involve breaking up a marriage or a family.

When you are involved with someone who drinks too much, you may be lucky and that person may change. Sometimes you may decide to accept things as they are, and one way of obtaining the help and strength to accomplish this may be through joining Al-Anon. If you have provided opportunities for change and this has not occurred, getting out of the relationship may be the best way to go, at least in the case of marital partners. Where it is your parent or your child who drinks too much, the equivalent of separation and divorce does not exist. Nevertheless, placing distance between yourself and the loved one (and here I mean emotional distance, rather than geographic) may be a very helpful thing to do. Ask yourself: "Is it possible that in some way I am facilitating the continued drinking of my loved one?" If need be, get some professional counseling to answer this question if you cannot answer it yourself. If you cannot afford or cannot obtain professional counseling, start attending meetings of Al-Anon, where eventually you will find the answer.

Sometimes I meet women who admit that their husband's excessive drinking was already known to them before marriage. However, they were in love and they listened to the promises about how the drinking would stop after the marriage. Such promises are invariably broken, and I merely wish to end this topic by saying that no one should ever marry someone with the objective of effecting change. The faithless boyfriend will be an unfaithful husband. The "playfully punching" boyfriend will be a wife beater, and the heavily drinking boyfriend will be a heavily drinking husband.

Dealing with a drunk person

There is no point in trying to reason or argue with a person who is drunk. The best approach may be to humor him. If he is still very active, loud, and perhaps argumentative, try to keep everyone, including yourself, as calm as possible. If you can get the drunk person to lie down and sleep, this will give his liver time to burn up the alcohol and enable him to become sober. There is nothing that you can give a drunk person that will safely sober him or her up more quickly. Trying to put him in a cold shower or walking him up and down is useless and may be hazardous.

Many heavy drinkers are also heavy smokers, and if the drunk person is trying to smoke, someone should stay in the vicinity to be certain that he does not pass out and set himself or the furniture on fire.

If a drunk person is very belligerent and is threatening or even attacking other people, it may well be necessary to get out of the way. Sometimes it will be necessary to call upon law enforcement officers for help.

Once a drunk person has fallen asleep, leave him alone as long as he is breathing peacefully and showing no signs of vomiting. If vomiting occurs in someone who is semi-stuporous, there is danger of getting solids and fluids sucked into the lungs. If such a person is lying down, he or she should be turned over, face down, with the head to one side to prevent choking. Don't try to give anything by mouth. If there is evidence that he or she is having breathing difficulty or is unconscious (unable to be aroused), or if there is suspicion that there may have been a blow to the head, seek medical help. Rather than calling a doctor to the home, a more useful tactic is to call the local rescue squad to get him to the emergency room of a hospital where medical help is available. The rescue squad vehicle carries emergency equipment and is operated by well-trained people who will know what to do.

Alcohol affects the ability of the body to maintain its normal temperature. Thus, a drunk person in a very hot environment will gradually become overheated. This brings about the danger of heat stroke, and thus, for example, heavy drinking at a football stadium while sitting in the sun on a hot day can be very dangerous. Equally dangerous is exposing the drunk person to excessive cold. Once he or she has gone to sleep, they should be covered lightly to help them to maintain body temperature. Some years ago in Greensboro, North Carolina, a group of people were drinking heavily and one man passed out. His drinking companions reasoned that he would sober up if put outside on the porch where it was cold. They themselves were drinking heavily which interferes with memory. Thus, they went to bed and forgot about him. The next morning, he was dead. His body temperature had gone down continuously during the night until his vital functions failed. Keep in mind, though, that people have recovered from severe drops in body temperature. Such a person should be rushed to the hospital even though apparently dead. Sometimes they can be revived.

A drunk person should not be allowed to get involved in a hazardous situation such as driving a car. Friends do not let friends drive home drunk. It is better for them to spend the night in your house or for you to drive them yourself or to call a taxi. There is nothing illegal about being drunk in a private home, and the police in many communities would prefer to be called to help to get someone to his own home rather than have to investigate the wreck that he caused while driving drunk.

Finally, keep in mind that there is no point in trying to reason or argue with a person while they are drunk, since they are not receptive at this time to any imploring you may do and they will forget it anyway. Talk about the episode when there is a chance that he or she will remember your discussion. In other words, wait until he is sober.

section four

SUPPLEMENTARY INFORMATION

section four

SUPPLEMENTARY

INFORMATION

chapter thirty-four

Further

Reading

Suggestions, and

Sources of Help

Frequently when I am quoted in the news media as having said something about alcohol or alcoholism, I receive a rash of telephone calls and letters asking for further information. This whole book contains a great deal of information, but for those who remain unsaturated, this chapter suggests other places to turn to.

In this chapter I suggest various books and pamphlets of a general nature about alcohol and alcoholism. The next section provides some specific references to expand on issues discussed in chapters of this book. Following that is a section listing various organizations for lay people and professionals that can provide information and sometimes other services in the general area of alcohol use and abuse. Finally, there is a section on how to find sources of help.

General books and pamphlets on alcohol and alcoholism

This book is designed for the average lay reader, but for anyone who wants more detailed information or access to scholarly references, the most suitable single source is a book edited by Beatrice Rouse and me and published in 1978, *Drinking: Alcohol in American Society—Issues and Current Research*, edited by J. A. Ewing and B. A. Rouse, published by Nelson-Hall of Chicago.

Here are some other sources of information:

Kissin, Benjamin, and Begleiter, Henri, eds. *Biochemistry*. The Biology of Alcoholism, Vol. 1. New York: Plenum Press, 1971.

————. *Physiology and Behavior*. The Biology of Alcoholism, Vol. 2. New York: Plenum Press, 1972.

————. *Clinical Pathology*. The Biology of Alcoholism, Vol. 3. New York: Plenum Press, 1974.

————. *Social Aspects of Alcoholism*. The Biology of Alcoholism, Vol. 4. New York: Plenum Press, 1976.

————. *Treatment and Rehabilitation of the Chronic Alcoholic*. The Biology of Alcoholism, Vol. 5. New York: Plenum Press, 1977.

Seixas, Frank A., ed. *Biological, Biochemical, and Clinical Studies*. Currents in Alcoholism, Vol. 1. New York: Grune and Stratton, 1977.

————. *Psychiatric, Psychological, Social, and Epidemiological Studies*. Currents in Alcoholism, Vol. 2. New York: Grune and Stratton, 1977.

————. *Biological, Biochemical, and Clinical Studies*. Currents in Alcoholism, Vol. 3. New York: Grune and Stratton, 1978.

————. *Psychiatric, Psychological, Social, and Epidemiological Studies*. Currents in Alcoholism, Vol. 4. New York: Grune and Stratton, 1979.

Galanter, Marc, ed. *Biomedical Issues and Clinical Effects of Alcoholism*. Currents in Alcoholism, Vol. 5. New York: Grune and Stratton, 1979.

Wallgren, Henrik, and Barry, Herbert, III. *Biochemical, Physiological and Psychological Aspects.* Actions of Alcohol, Vol. 1. New York: Elsevier Publishing, 1970.

————. *Chronic and Clinical Aspects.* Actions of Alcohol, Vol. 2. New York: Elsevier Publishing, 1970.

Government sponsored sources of material are as follows:

National Clearinghouse for Alcohol Information
Box 2345
Rockville, Maryland 20852

In Canada the Province of Ontario has a splendid organization:

Addiction Research Foundation
33 Russell Street
Toronto, Ontario, Canada M5S 2S1

The Rutgers Center of Alcohol Studies has a huge collection of abstracts and articles on all aspects of this subject in addition to publishing the monthly *Journal of Studies on Alcohol.* It is possible to negotiate with them directly or through your local librarian. If you have a specific area of inquiry, you can make a long-distance computer search of the stored materials from a scientific library. Their address is:

The Center of Alcohol Studies
Rutgers, The State University of New Jersey
P.O. Box 969
Piscataway, New Jersey 08854

The privately supported National Council on Alcoholism has a publications department that will be happy to send you their current catalogue of various educational materials. Write to:

Publications Department
National Council on Alcoholism, Inc.
733 Third Avenue
New York, NY 10017

The Hazelden Foundation in Minnesota has an excellent literature department that can supply what is current in the field. Write to:

> Hazelden Literature Department
> Hazelden Foundation
> Box 176
> Center City, MN 55012

The Hazelden Foundation Literature Department can also be reached through a toll-free telephone number: 800-328-9288.

Free pamphlets and other informational items that have a specific point of view are available from:

> Distilled Spirits Council of the United States, Inc.
> 1300 Pennsylvania Building
> Washington, D.C. 20004

Pamphlets about alcohol and alcoholism are available for bulk purchase from:

> Channing L. Beete, Inc.
> 45 Federal Street
> Greenfield, MA 01301

The Raleigh Hills Foundation has begun a monthly newsletter of "Advances in Alcoholism." This is prepared and edited by the Alcohol and Drug Abuse Research Center of Harvard Medical School and the McLean Hospital of Massachusetts. It is available for $10 annually by writing:

> The Raleigh Hills Foundation
> 881 Dover Drive, Suite 20
> Newport Beach, CA 92663

For physicians, a publication called *Alcoholism Up-date* is published by Ayerst Laboratories and focuses on current approaches to the management and rehabilitation of the problem drinker. Physicians who want to get on the mailing list should write to:

Alcoholism Up-date
Ayerst Laboratories
685 Third Avenue
New York, NY 10017

The Christopher D. Smithers Foundation, Inc. is an organization that promotes education as well as research and treatment in alcoholism. For a pricelist of publications write to:

The Christopher D. Smithers Foundation, Inc.
41 East 57 Street
New York, NY 10022

For literature about Alcoholics Anonymous you can contact your local AA groups or write to:

Alcoholics Anonymous
Box 459
Grand Central Station
New York, NY 10017

Those seeking literature on the subject of Al-Anon and Alateen can obtain an order blank by writing to:

Al-Anon Family Group Headquarters, Inc.
P.O. Box 182
Madison Square Station
New York, NY 10010

Sources on special issues

The sources listed above can provide any additional reading that anyone might want to do about topics that are covered in Section I of this book. However, there are some additional sources of a more specialized nature.

FOR CHILDREN. Judith S. Seixas has written two books that are specifically addressed to children. The first, entitled *Alcohol—What It Is—What It Does,* is an introduction for children aged 6 to 9 years. Another of her publications is called, *Living With a Parent Who Drinks Too Much.* These books are available through the National Council on Alcoholism, whose address is listed above.

ON FETAL ALCOHOL SYNDROME. Research on the fetal alcohol syndrome is still going on and much remains to be learned. The National Institute on Alcohol Abuse and Alcoholism, 5600 Fishers Lane, Rockville, MD 20857 has a publication called *Alcohol and Your Unborn Baby,* that undoubtedly will be updated as information is gathered. An entire book on the subject is, *Just So It's Healthy,* by Lucy Barry Robe; it is available through the National Council on Alcoholism.

HISTORICAL. An important book that supplies much historical information about drinking in North America is *Drunken Comportment: A Social Explanation,* by Craig MacAndrew and Robert B. Edgerton, Aldine Publishing Co., Chicago, 1969.

ON CONTROLLING DRINKING. Anyone who decides to work hard at reducing his or her drinking and who wants more suggestions than this book provides should obtain *How to Control Your Drinking,* by William R. Miller and Ricardo F. Muñoz, Prentice-Hall, Inc., New Jersey, 1976.

ON CHOOSING TREATMENT. In Chapter 26 I mentioned my article on the importance of offering a choice of treatments. It is: "Matching Therapy and Patients: The Cafeteria Plan," by John A. Ewing, published in *British Journal of Addiction,* 72:13–18, 1977.

ON WOMEN AND MINORITIES. For women there is a pamphlet entitled *Alcohol Abuse and Women—A Guide to Getting Help,* available from the National Institute on Alcohol Abuse and Alcoholism, 5600 Fishers Lane, Rockville, MD 20857. Another book obtainable through the National Council on Alcoholism is entitled, *A Dangerous Pleasure: Alcohol From the Woman's Perspective—It's Effect on Body, Mind, and Relationships,* by Geraldine Youcha.

The National Institute on Alcohol Abuse and Alcoholism has various pamphlets on minorities and alcohol such as, *The Unseen Crisis, Blacks and Alcohol.* Some of their publications can also be obtained in Spanish.

WRITERS AND ALCOHOLISM. In Chapter 21 I referred to some publications by Dr. Donald W. Goodwin on writers and alcoholism. Here are the references:

Goodwin, Donald W. "The Alcoholism of F. Scott Fitzgerald." In *Journal of the American Medical Association,* 212 (April 6, 1970): 86–90.

――――. "The Alcoholism of Eugene O'Neill," In *Journal of the American Medical Association,* 216 (April 5, 1971): 99–104.

――――. "The Muse and the Martini," (about Georges Simenon). In *Journal of the American Medical Association,* 224 (April 2, 1973): 35–38.

Organizations concerned with alcohol and alcoholism

FOR LAY PERSONS

The National Council on Alcoholism, Inc. is the national voluntary health agency founded to combat the disease of alcoholism. It is completely independent of Alcoholics Anonymous and its major areas of activity are medical, labor-management, prevention and education, public information, publications, research and evaluation, community services, women, youth, the family, and minority affairs programs. I already have referred to its publication services; affiliates of the National Council are found throughout the United States as local Councils. There are medical, nursing, and research components that will be referred to in the section for professionals.

Alcoholics Anonymous is the organization for people who suffer from alcoholism and desire to stop drinking, and Al-Anon and Alateen are for their family members and friends. Addresses of both organizations have already been provided on page 195.

There are some organizations that are devoted to helping

their members to drink in a responsible and less unhealthy manner. Please note that this is not the recommended treatment for a person suffering from alcoholism. However, for the person who is not a primary alcoholic and has grown careless in his or her drinking habits, membership in one of these organizations can prove very helpful. One of the earliest such groups that I know of called themselves "Drinkwatchers."

A newer organization on the West Coast is called "Responsible Drinkers" and bills itself as a nonprofit organization dedicated to the principle of alcohol abuse avoidance. Their address is:

> Responsible Drinkers, Inc.
> P.O. Box 1062
> Burlingame, CA 94010

They publish a newsletter and hold local chapter meetings.

A group called "Women for Sobriety, Inc." offers membership and help to women who have a drinking problem. They publish a monthly newsletter called "Sobering Thoughts." In addition, they produce other publications and provide help to anyone interested in getting a Women for Sobriety group started. Their address is:

> Women for Sobriety, Inc.
> P.O. Box 618
> Quakertown, PA 18951

I hope that this book has made it clear that many nonalcoholics (spouse, children, parents, grandparents, in-laws, friends, etc.) suffer from the effects of alcoholism in some way. Such people may wish to join the Other Victims of Alcoholism, Inc., which publishes a quarterly entitled *The Other Side of the Coin*. You can also write to them and request their order form for books, cassette tapes, posters, and pamphlets. Their address is:

> Other Victims of Alcoholism, Inc.
> P.O. Box 921
> Radio City Station
> New York, NY 10019

A pamphlet entitled *The Homosexual Alcoholic* is available for 25¢ by writing to:

Tucker
P.O. Box 4623
Arlington, VA 22204

The same source can provide a listing of facilities and services for gay alcoholics and drug abusers for $1. Also available from that source are directories of gay groups of Alcoholics Anonymous and Al-Anon; these are available only to members of Alcoholics Anonymous and Alcoholics Together (which uses the AA program for recovery, but whose meetings are open only to gays), and to members of Al-Anon. It is not necessary to be gay to receive either of these directories, but it is necessary, "for reasons of anonymity and double confidentiality" to be a member of Alcoholics Anonymous, Alcoholics Together, or Al-Anon.

For Professionals

Alcoholics Anonymous publishes a brochure, *AA Wants to Work With You.* for doctors, clergymen, psychologists, counselors, social workers, armed forces commanders, and others who need to know about the organization. They also publish a newsletter for professional men and women called *About AA.* Those who wish to receive either should write to Box 459 at Grand Central Station, New York, NY 10017.

The National Council on Alcoholism has three professional component societies. The American Medical Society on Alcoholism (AMSA) is a national organization of over 1,200 physicians with special interest and experience in the field of alcoholism who wish to share this experience with the general public. AMSA publishes a journal called *Alcoholism: Clinical and Experimental Research.* Applications for membership can be sent to the New York address of the National Council on Alcoholism. Many states also have state groups of AMSA.

Another NCA component is the Research Society on Alcoholism (RSA), which serves as a meeting ground for research scientists working in the area of alcoholism and alcohol related problems. Some M.D.s belong to the RSA, but this component has many research scientist members whose doctorates are in subjects other than medicine. The official journal of the society is *Alcoholism: Clinical and Experimental Research.*

Finally, there is the National Nurses Society on Alcoholism (NNSA), which is a national organization that serves as a forum for nurses interested in the disease of alcoholism to extend knowledge in this field, promote the dissemination of that knowledge, and enlighten and direct public opinion in regard to alcoholism.

There are many other organizations for professionals who will normally align themselves with people working in the same field. Some examples:

> Association of Labor-Management Administrators and Consultants on Alcoholism, Inc.
> Suite 907
> 1800 North Kent Street
> Arlington, VA 22209

> National Association of Gay Alcoholism Professionals
> P.O. Box 376
> Oakland, NJ 07436

The above listings are by no means comprehensive. In many states there are state-wide or local organizations for special groups such as "Alcoholism Professionals" or alcoholism counselors, educators, and others.

How to find help

As I have indicated elsewhere in this book, help is available for anyone who will look for it. Consult both the regular telephone directory and the Yellow Pages if you are looking for assistance in "drying out" or treatment either on an outpatient or an institutional basis. Talk with your doctor, your minister, your attorney, or your neighbor. Many people know what is available locally and regionally. Directories of treatment facilities with details of costs and admission procedures are often published by state organizations or branches of State government. Some national directories have been published from time to time, but these rapidly go out of date. Suggestions were provided in Chapter 26 for getting help with a drinking problem and details about Alcoholics Anonymous are to be found in Chapter 32. Your local library will also be a source of much useful information if you just ask. Consider also a phone call to your local Public Health Department or Social Services Department. Frankly, if you have read this book and followed its suggestions and still feel unable to reach help, it may be because you are not yet ready to try hard enough to get it.

Finally, if you really are at a loss for some piece of information or a reference to a source in the scientific literature, we will try to help you at the University of North Carolina Center for Alcohol Studies. Please make your question or request as clear and short as possible and enclose a check or cash for $1 in order to help to defray our printing and mailing costs. We can supply you with a list of available publications (including most of my own contributions to the scientific literature), and if there are some of these that you wish to order, they can be provided for the cost of copying. For the quickest possible response, do not write to me but write to:

The Librarian
Center for Alcohol Studies
School of Medicine
Building 207H
Chapel Hill, NC 27514

chapter thirty-five

Questionnaires

to Detect

Problem

Drinking

I hope that the earlier sections of this book have demonstrated that the answer or answers to one or a series of questions cannot in any absolute way define the presence or absence of alcoholism. However, such questions can stimulate some self-examination and may, either immediately or later, create an adequate level of awareness in any one individual. These questionnaires have helped others to recognize what was happening to them. Please do not use them as party games. They should be considered seriously by one person alone or in the presence of a spouse, friend, or counselor in a thoroughly sober and serious atmosphere.

The National Council on Alcoholism lists what they call

"early warning signals" which, although not in questionnaire form, may be useful. They are:

1. Difficult to get along with when drinking.
2. Drinks "because depressed."
3. Drinks "to calm nerves."
4. Drinks until "dead drunk" at times.
5. Can't remember parts of some drinking episodes.
6. Hides liquor.
7. Lies about drinking.
8. Neglects to eat when drinking.
9. Neglects family when drinking.

Ayerst Laboratories publishes a useful little booklet that I often go over with patient and spouse in my office. The questions fall into three groups.

Early Symptoms (the first stage of alcoholism)

- Are you beginning to lie or feel guilty about your drinking?
- Do you gulp your drinks?
- Do you try to have a few extra drinks before joining others drinking?
- Must you drink at certain times—for example before lunch or a special event; after a disappointment or quarrel?
- Do you drink because you feel tired, depressed, or worried?
- Are you annoyed when family or friends talk to you about your drinking?
- Are you beginning to have memory blackouts and occasional passouts?

Middle Symptoms

- Are you making more promises and telling more lies about your drinking?
- Are there more times when you need a drink?

- When sober, do you regret what you have said or done while drinking?
- Are you drinking more often alone, avoiding family or close friends?
- Do you have weekend drinking bouts and Monday hangovers?
- Have you been going "on the wagon" to control your drinking?
- Are memory blackouts and passouts becoming more frequent?

The questions that detect the late symptoms (the advanced stage of alcoholism) are as follows:

Late Symptoms (advanced alcoholism)

- Do you drink to live and live to drink?
- Are you noticeably drunk on important occasions—for example, a special dinner or meeting?
- Do your drinking bouts last for several days at a time?
- Do you sometimes get "the shakes" in the morning and take "a quick one"?
- Do blackouts and passouts now happen very often?
- Have you lost concern for your family and others around you?

Some questionnaires aimed at problem drinking simply stir up more guilt in the problem drinker. They use phrases such as "failing to keep promises" and "neglecting your family." The list of questions provided by Alcoholics Anonymous is less accusatory:

1. Have you ever tried to stop drinking for a week (or longer), only to fall short of your goal?
2. Do you resent the advice of others who try to get you to stop drinking?
3. Have you ever tried to control your drinking by switching from one alcoholic beverage to another?
4. Have you ever taken a morning drink during the past year?
5. Do you envy people who can drink without getting into trouble?

6. Has your drinking problem become progressively more serious during the past year?

7. Has your drinking created problems at home?

8. At social affairs where drinking is limited, do you try to obtain "extra" drinks?

9. Despite evidence to the contrary, have you continued to assert that you can stop drinking "on your own" whenever you wish?

10. During the past year, have you missed time from work as a result of drinking?

11. Have you ever "blacked out" during your drinking?

12. Have you ever felt you could do more with your life if you did not drink?*

A newspaper article published widely throughout the country in April of 1979 quoted from the April issue of *Harper's Bazaar.* The article was on the subject of alcoholism among women and reported that working women are more vulnerable to alcoholism than others. The following is a questionnaire entitled "Are you a Problem Drinker?" specifically directed at women.

1. Do you occasionally drink heavily after a disappointment, a quarrel, or when the boss gives you a hard time?

2. When you have trouble or feel under pressure, do you always drink more heavily than usual?

3. Have you noticed that you are able to handle more liquor than you did when you were first drinking?

4. Did you ever wake up on the "morning after" and discover that you could not remember part of the evening before, even though your friends tell you that you did not "pass out?"

5. When drinking with other people, do you try to have a few extra drinks when others will not know it?

6. Are there certain occasions when you feel uncomfortable if alcohol is not available?

*The 12 questions from "Is A.A. for You?" are reprinted with permission of A.A. World Services, Inc.

7. Have you recently noticed that when you begin drinking you are in more of a hurry to get the first drink than you used to be?

8. Do you sometimes feel a little guilty about your drinking?

9. Are you secretly irritated when your family or friends discuss your drinking?

10. Have you recently noticed an increase in the frequency of your memory "blackouts?"

11. Do you often find that you wish to continue drinking after your friends say they have had enough?

12. Do you usually have a reason for the occasions when you drink heavily?

13. When you are sober, do you often regret things you have done or said while drinking?

14. Have you tried switching brands or following different plans for controlling your drinking?

15. Have you often failed to keep the promises you have made to yourself about controlling or cutting down on your drinking?

16. Have you ever tried to control your drinking by making a change in jobs, or moving to a new location?

17. Do you try to avoid family or close friends while you are drinking?

18. Are you having an increasing number of financial and work problems?

19. Do more people seem to be treating you unfairly without good reason?

20. Do you eat very little or irregularly when you are drinking?

21. Do you sometimes have the "shakes" in the morning and find that it helps to have a little drink?

22. Have you recently noticed that you cannot drink as much as you once did?

23. Do you sometimes stay drunk for several days at a time?

24. Do you sometimes feel very depressed and wonder whether life is worth living?

25. Sometimes after periods of drinking, do you see or hear things that aren't there?

26.   Do you get terribly frightened after you have been drinking heavily?*

If you answered "yes" to any of the questions, you have some of the symptoms that may indicate alcoholism.

"Yes" answers to several of the questions indicate the following stages of alcoholism: Questions 1–8, early stage; Questions 9–21, middle stage; Questions 22–26, the beginning of the final stage.

Drs. Wendell M. Swenson and Robert M. Morse of the Mayo Clinic have developed a self-administered alcoholism screening test (SAAST) which has been used with both alcoholic patients and spouses. Note that the plus sign indicates that the average alcoholic answers "yes" to the question and the minus sign indicates that he or she will answer "no." Here are the 34 questions:

1.+   Do you enjoy a drink now and then? (If you never drink alcoholic beverages, and have no previous experience with drinking, do not continue with questionnaire.)

2.–   Do you feel you are a normal drinker? (That is, drink no more than average.)

3.+   Have you ever awakened the morning after some drinking the night before and found that you could not remember a part of the evening?

4.+   Do close relatives ever worry or complain about your drinking?

5.–   Can you stop drinking without a struggle after one or two drinks?

6.+   Do you ever feel guilty about your drinking?

7.–   Do friends or relatives think you are a normal drinker?

8.–   Are you always able to stop drinking when you want to?

9.+   Have you ever attended a meeting of Alcoholics Anonymous (AA) because of your drinking?

10.+   Have you gotten into physical fights when drinking?

*Courtesy of *Harper's Bazaar.* Copyright © 1979 The Hearst Corporation. Developed by the National Council on Alcoholism.

11.+ Has drinking ever created problems between you and your wife, husband, parent, or near relative?

12.+ Has your wife, husband, or other family member ever gone to anyone for help about your drinking?

13.+ Have you ever lost friendships because of your drinking?

14.+ Have you ever gotten into trouble at work because of drinking?

15.+ Have you ever lost a job because of drinking?

16.+ Have you ever neglected your obligations, your family, or your work for 2 or more days in a row because you were drinking?

17.+ Do you ever drink in the morning?

18.+ Have you ever felt the need to cut down on your drinking?

19.+ Have there been times in your adult life when you have found it necessary to completely avoid alcohol?

20.+ Have you ever been told you have liver trouble? Cirrhosis?

21.+ Have you ever had delirium tremens (DTs)?

22.+ Have you ever had severe shaking, heard voices, or seen things that weren't there after heavy drinking?

23.+ Have you ever gone to anyone for help about your drinking?

24.+ Have you ever been in a hospital because of drinking?

25.+ Have you ever been told by a doctor to stop drinking?

26.+ Have you ever been a patient in a psychiatric hospital or on a psychiatric ward of a general hospital?

27.+ Was drinking part of the problem that resulted in that hospitalization?

28.+ Have you ever been a patient at a psychiatric or mental health clinic or gone to any doctor, social worker, or clergyman for help with any emotional problem?

29.+ Have you ever been arrested, even for a few hours, because of drunken behavior (not driving)? How many times?_____

30.+ Have you ever been arrested, even for a few hours, because of driving while intoxicated? How many times?_____

31–34. Have any of the following relatives ever had problems with alcohol?

31.+   A. Parents

32.+   B. Brothers or sisters

33.+   C. Husband or wife

34.+   D. Children

A total score of 10 or more alcoholic responses indicates probable alcoholism. Scores of 7 and 8 suggest the strong possibility of alcoholism.

Of course, there are other questionnaires that have been developed for people to administer to themselves about their drinking. However, I think that the above examples will suffice.

A problem area is the questions that doctors should ask their patients about their drinking. As I have indicated elsewhere in this book, doctors are not always successful in getting their patients to talk about their drinking. This may be, in fact, because doctors are notoriously careless in asking appropriate questions about alcohol and drug use. To some extent this is based upon the fact that doctors are themselves alcohol (and therefore drug) users. A doctor may be not the least embarrassed to ask a patient about whether or not he has had various venereal diseases, and may then say something like, "I suppose you're a social drinker," instead of giving the patient the chance to report his or her use of alcohol. An article published in the August 10, 1979 issue of the *Journal of the American Medical Association* demonstrated that the majority of drug and alcohol abusers acknowledged the existence of their problem on a short questionnaire that was part of a medical intake form. This came from a study by Drs. F. S. Tennant, J. T. Ungerleider, and Ms. C. M. Day. The checklist they provided simply included phrases like "alcohol problem" and "drug abuse." A similar experience has been reported by Dr. Charles Whitfield, who is an internist who specializes in dealing with alcohol problems and alcoholism. He reports that he asks his patients: "How do you use alcohol?" He goes on to ask, "Have you ever wondered if drinking might be bad for you?" The next question is something such as, "Do you wonder if you might be alcoholic?" Dr. Whitfield asks the patient who wonders if he might be an alcoholic to indicate what he believes an alcoholic to be. Once the patient gives his definition or explanation, Dr. Whitfield asks, "Do you think you fit any of these definitions?"

The point is, that often patients want doctors to explore these issues with them and, given the opportunity, they will prove to be more honest than the doctor expects.

About ten years ago, Beatrice Rouse, Dr. William E. Bakewell and I experimented in a variety of clinical settings with various questionnaires that had been developed for detection of alcoholism in a medical setting. Most questionnaires duplicate each other by using different words to detect similar patterns of behavior. We found that we could eliminate many questions and that we were left with four that were particularly "powerful" in detecting problems with alcohol. The first deals with the alcoholic's common problem of repeatedly trying to get the drinking under control only to lose control again and again once he resumes drinking. The next detects sensitivity of the alcoholic to outside criticism of his drinking behavior. This is not surprising, since he already feels quite guilty about his inability to control his drinking and, therefore, comments from others hit a tender spot. The third question taps into the personal sense of guilt, and the fourth one looks at the tendency to use morning drinking as a remedy for excessive drinking the night before.

From these questions I developed the mnemonic "CAGE" by rearranging the questions shown below:

The CAGE Questions
1. Have you felt the need to   **C**ut down your drinking?
2. Have you ever felt   **A**nnoyed by criticism of your drinking?
3. Have you had   **G**uilt feelings about drinking?
4. Do you ever take a morning   **E**ye-opener?

Quite a few normal drinkers have felt the need to cut down their drinking from time to time, perhaps because of excessive weight gain or for some other reason. However, they report that once they have cut down their drinking, it stays cut down. This of course is not the alcoholic's drinking pattern. Few people other than alcoholics feel annoyed by people's criticism of their drinking. About 10 percent of the general population report some guilt feelings about drinking, particularly if they were raised in an abstaining household and have any religious or other doubts about whether or not they should drink. Finally, taking a morning eye-opener is virtually the exclusive drinking pattern of the alcoholic.

I have been trying to encourage physicians to use the CAGE questions routinely as part of their overall examination of substance use that includes how much the patient uses tobacco, caffeine, prescription and nonprescription drugs. Even if the patient does not immediately consent to stop drinking when confronted with the existence of a drinking problem, the doctor should know that the process has been set in motion that will, in most cases, eventually lead to decisions to get the alcoholism under control. Of course, the doctor will not always succeed; some patients seem inevitably determined to drink themselves to death. However, a sympathetic and understanding physician who focuses on health issues and remains steadfastly available is likely to help in the long run.

chapter thirty- six

Keeping

a Drinking

Diary

If you want to calculate the approximate level of alcohol reached in your blood for any one drinking experience you need to use the formula that takes into account body weight, alcohol consumed, and the passage of time as shown in Table 4-1 on page 23.

The Drinking Diary, on the other hand, is aimed at enabling you to record your average consumption of alcoholic beverages over days, weeks, and months. This enables you to get some idea as to the amounts you are consuming, which can then be compared with the information in this book about what are considered hazardous levels of drinking. Another useful function of the Diary can be to compare your alcohol consumption now to your alcohol consumption one year from now, or ten years from now. An honest use of the Drinking Diary will enable you to see if your consumption is increasing over time.

To keep it simple, it is best just to record "drinks consumed," but this requires either marking them down as soon as they are poured or remembering exactly how many you had. You also must know equivalents, so that equivalent drinks can be recorded. Note the following table:

DRINKS WITH APPROXIMATELY EQUAL ALCOHOL
12 ounces of beer
4 ounces of table wine (red, white, rosé)
2½ ounces of fortified wine (sherry, Port)
1¼ ounces of 86 proof spirits
1 ounce of 100 proof spirits

Each of the above drinks is approximately equal to any of the others in terms of alcohol content and each can be recorded as one drink. Thus, if you are pouring, and measuring, larger amounts, these can be recorded as 1½ or 2 drinks, as appropriate.

If you are using the Drinking Diary to calculate the total number of grams of alcohol consumed on a daily basis, you can consider that each of the drinks listed above contains 12 grams of alcohol.

You can start keeping a Drinking Diary at any time. Write in the month at the top of the page and go to the line for the day when you are starting. All you need to do now is pencil in a mark for each drink you consume. It is then easy to find the daily, weekly, or monthly totals.

Month of _____	Daily Total	Weekly Total	Month of _____	Daily Total	Weekly Total
Day			Day		
1			1		
2			2		
3			3		
4			4		
5			5		
6			6		
7			7		
8			8		
9			9		
10			10		
11			11		
12			12		
13			13		
14			14		
15			15		
16			16		
17			17		
18			18		
19			19		
20			20		
21			21		
22			22		
23			23		
24			24		
25			25		
26			26		
27			27		
28			28		
29			29		
30			30		
31			31		

Monthly Total:_____   Monthly Total:_____

Month of _____			Month of _____		
Day	Daily Total	Weekly Total	Day	Daily Total	Weekly Total
1			1		
2			2		
3			3		
4			4		
5			5		
6			6		
7			7		
8			8		
9			9		
10			10		
11			11		
12			12		
13			13		
14			14		
15			15		
16			16		
17			17		
18			18		
19			19		
20			20		
21			21		
22			22		
23			23		
24			24		
25			25		
26			26		
27			27		
28			28		
29			29		
30			30		
31			31		

Monthly Total:_____   Monthly Total:_____

Month of _____			Month of _____		
Day	Daily Total	Weekly Total	Day	Daily Total	Weekly Total
1			1		
2			2		
3			3		
4			4		
5			5		
6			6		
7			7		
8			8		
9			9		
10			10		
11			11		
12			12		
13			13		
14			14		
15			15		
16			16		
17			17		
18			18		
19			19		
20			20		
21			21		
22			22		
23			23		
24			24		
25			25		
26			26		
27			27		
28			28		
29			29		
30			30		
31			31		

Monthly Total:_____   Monthly Total:_____

Month of _____			Month of _____		
Day	Daily Total	Weekly Total	Day	Daily Total	Weekly Total
1			1		
2			2		
3			3		
4			4		
5			5		
6			6		
7			7		
8			8		
9			9		
10			10		
11			11		
12			12		
13			13		
14			14		
15			15		
16			16		
17			17		
18			18		
19			19		
20			20		
21			21		
22			22		
23			23		
24			24		
25			25		
26			26		
27			27		
28			28		
29			29		
30			30		
31			31		

Monthly Total:_____   Monthly Total:_____

Month of _____			Month of _____		
Day	Daily Total	Weekly Total	Day	Daily Total	Weekly Total
1			1		
2			2		
3			3		
4			4		
5			5		
6			6		
7			7		
8			8		
9			9		
10			10		
11			11		
12			12		
13			13		
14			14		
15			15		
16			16		
17			17		
18			18		
19			19		
20			20		
21			21		
22			22		
23			23		
24			24		
25			25		
26			26		
27			27		
28			28		
29			29		
30			30		
31			31		

Monthly Total:_____   Monthly Total:_____

| Month of _____ | | | Month of _____ | | |
Day	Daily Total	Weekly Total	Day	Daily Total	Weekly Total
1			1		
2			2		
3			3		
4			4		
5			5		
6			6		
7			7		
8			8		
9			9		
10			10		
11			11		
12			12		
13			13		
14			14		
15			15		
16			16		
17			17		
18			18		
19			19		
20			20		
21			21		
22			22		
23			23		
24			24		
25			25		
26			26		
27			27		
28			28		
29			29		
30			30		
31			31		

Monthly Total:_____   Monthly Total:_____

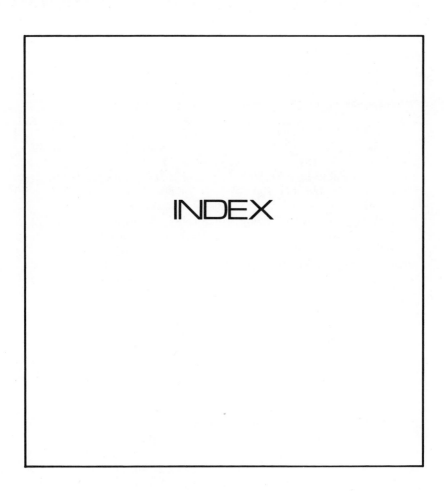

INDEX